THE WRITING CIRCLE

A Guide for Writers and Peer Readers

Second Edition

Dick Harrington

Piedmont Virginia Community College

HARCOURT
BRACE

HARCOURT BRACE COLLEGE PUBLISHERS

Fort Worth   Philadelphia   San Diego   New York   Orlando   Austin   San Antonio
Toronto   Montreal   London   Sydney   Tokyo

ISBN: 0-15-508-164-0

Address for orders:
Harcourt Brace College Publishers
6277 Sea Harbor Drive
Orlando, Florida 32887-6777
1-800-782-4479

Address for editorial correspondence:
Harcourt Brace College Publishers
301 Commerce Street, Suite 3700
Fort Worth, Texas 76102

Web site address:
http://www.harbrace.com/english

PRINTED IN THE UNITED STATES OF AMERICA.
890123456 023 98765432

To the Student

My wife Victoria and I live in a timber-frame house perched on the mountainside of Virginia's Blue Ridge just below the Appalachian Trail and Blue Ridge Parkway. Our driveway is steep, and in winter when it snows, I clear it with a snowblower that attaches to the front of our Gravely tractor. Otherwise we'd be snowed in up here. The winters are relatively mild compared, say, to Minnesota, but we do get some pretty good snows. To keep the snowblower and tractor in good working order, I make periodic adjustments and repairs (though for major work I call the tractor mechanic on the other side of the mountain.) I'm just so-so as a mechanic. In order to work on the stuff, I need something to go by, a handbook. Fortunately, Gravely provided me with one for the tractor and one for the snowblower. When I can't figure out what to do on my own, I get out the manual and follow the directions, written and illustrated clearly so I can usually get the job done.

I've written this book to guide you, I hope clearly, in something much more complex than working on a snowblower. It's a handbook on working productively in small critique groups to help you and your classmates develop as college writers. I know of no better way to learn writing than to read one another's work in progress and respond constructively. Doing so takes gumption and training. It's pretty easy to read someone's draft and say, "It's good. I like it," or "It needs a lot of work, but I'm not sure what to tell you."

What's hard—and useful—is learning to talk about writing to help each writer want to improve and see ways of improving. What's also hard—and useful—is learning to talk regularly about the group as a group, learning to resolve any tension or other issue with civility. I want the book to help you make writing and each group session productive and satisfying for all. You can read it for background beforehand. And you can turn to it, as a handbook, for suggestions as you write alone and for specific procedures as you join your peers in a group session at a given stage of writing. It's a companion to your other books in the course—your writing handbook, your collection of readings, your dictionary, whatever books your instructor and/or English department have selected. Drawn from over three decades of teaching and research, it's been a labor of inquiry, devotion, and sweat. I hope it serves you as you step into your life as a college writer.

To the Instructor

In thirty years we've transformed the teaching and learning of writing. We can expect better writing from greater numbers of students because we now dare to coach them in both methods of composition and methods of collaboration. Guiding them through "stages" of writing enables them to refine their own methods and experiment with new methods, while emphasizing certain thinking tasks—and not others—at a given period of work. Collaboration with classmates offers what the instructor alone simply cannot provide: numerous readers and, more importantly, numerous responders. In a class period of, say, fifty minutes, four students in a critique group can experience four pieces of writing in progress as well as four responses to each—responses that generate possibilities for significant exploring, redrafting, refining, or proofing—depending upon the "stage" of focus. Such can happen in nearly any group if students are well trained in systematic yet natural methods of interacting about writing.

No pedagogy I've ever tried compares. When a particular group fails at a given task, it's usually because I've failed in training and coaching—failed to demonstrate adequately the type of response I expect, failed to include adequate practice, failed to provide written instructions and follow-up. Colleagues from various universities and colleges report that, while they believe in the value of critique groups, most of their students know little about discussing writing productively, and they as instructors feel uncertain how to guide them. Hence I offer this book as a guide to instructors as well as students.

Developed from my own practices with students as well as years of other research, it provides rationale, illustration, and specific directions for group work at each "stage." In my own classes, in both semesters of composition, I schedule four group sessions for each shorter paper—two at the stage of establishing a sound working draft, one at the stage of refining style, and one at the stage of proofing. I schedule more sessions for a longer paper. Instructions are unique to each stage. The book is designed as a manual. Before a given session, students can study appropriate chapters on rationale and procedures. Then to guide them during a session, they can turn to particular instructions. The primary features of each stage as well as the specific procedures are boxed for easy reference.

Because it's so difficult learning to respond productively, especially in the drafting stage, I recommend lots of modeling and practice as well as ongoing coaching during scheduled sessions. Unstaged videotapes of students in action help other students, as well as colleagues, see what's expected and possible. Videos also help my students and me learn what's working and what's not. I'm seeking ways to simplify the taping process so I can tape each group more often without impeding their work. The scenarios in the book illustrating student conversation are recreated from my study of videotapes and groups in person. With but one exception, the sample student drafts and responses are typed directly from the work of actual students, who graciously allowed me to include it. The one exception is Francesca Jones and her brainstorming, fastwriting, and outline—which I made up lock, stock, and barrel.

A writing group can be—and I believe should be—a support network that extends beyond the classroom. I've included a suggestion of partnership and mutual coaching whereby a pair of students can guide and support each other. Such a system is especially useful to non-residential students but applicable to all. First-year college writing is usually a required course with expectations far beyond what many students anticipate when they enter. A coaching call or visit with a peer can be invaluable, especially when the writing isn't going well—or isn't going at all. I also recommend each group of four select a group leader—to help interpret instructions, keep the group on task, ensure use of guidelines, serve as liaison with the instructor, help repair breakdowns, and the like. (The position might rotate so that every member gains leadership experience.) Each group might also select an advocate to work in tandem with the leader when breakdowns occur. The leader talks constructively with the one who has apparently breached the guidelines and aroused tension. The advocate also helps restore civility by working with the person who feels on the defensive. Much research on collaborative learning suggests that groups not only must employ such roles but also must discuss regularly and honestly how the group is doing as a group. The book offers guidance, including illustrative scenarios, for doing so.

Because composing and collaborating go hand in hand, I've included much on the writer's solitary work—exploring, drafting, refining, and proofing—entwined, I hope clearly, with rationale, specific procedures, and suggestions for working together with peers and with you as the instructor. Here and there I explain what I do in various situations while my students work in groups—to clarify for student readers the instructor's probable roles in relation to theirs. I also include brief introductions to writing and collaborating on the computer. Because methods, facilities, and programs vary so much, I indicate that the instructor will supply details regarding local practice.

You'll notice that my method for responding at the drafting stage involves two class periods and a fairly extensive assignment in between. In Session #1 each writer reads his or her draft aloud before supplying copies to the others. They listen, make notes, and then spend five minutes fastwriting their first impressions. After this process is complete for each writer, the writers hand out copies of their drafts. By the next period each responder fastwrites a 500-word response, generated by a heuristic, to each of three drafts. In Session #2 each responder presents orally for three minutes, using the written response as a guide. The writer listens and makes notes. After this process is complete for each writer, the responders give their written responses to the appropriate writers. For several years I'd tried teaching students to respond orally immediately after hearing a draft read aloud. Hard as they tried, with or without copies of the draft, many weren't able to give adequate responses in so little time. My current students learn to embrace the demanding, intense work of responding first in writing and then orally, because they experience how much it helps them read insightfully and interact usefully. I count their written responses as journal entries.

By the way, I refer to us interchangeably as professor, instructor, and teacher. We're allies in writing and teaching writing. I hope this little book adds something useful to your bag of pedagogy. In any case, I'd be delighted to hear from you.

Acknowledgements

To my students these past thirty years at Piedmont Virginia Community College, the University of Virginia, and Saint Paul's College for teaching me nearly everything I've learned about writing and the teaching of writing.

To the people at Harcourt Brace, especially sales representative Pauline Mula for professionalism and caring in initiating the project and supporting me; executive editor Michael Rosenberg for vision and diplomacy; and developmental editor Michell Phifer for graciousness and skill in seeing the project through.

To my friends and colleagues at Piedmont Virginia Community College—too numerous to name—for twenty-five years of comradeship in learning and teaching; for a cornucopia of technical support; for nurture, challenge, and inspiration; and for released time.

To Carol Pope and Joe Strzepek for years of learning and teaching together in the Central Virginia Writing Project. If not for you, I wouldn't know a lick about writing groups.

To all in the Two-Year College English Association—Southeast for living the spirit of what we do. Likewise to the Virginia Community Colleges Association.

To Margaret Aldridge, Houston Baker, Lester Beaurline, Randy Beckham, Ray Bratton, James Britten, Jeanette Cole, Brian Delaney, Deborah DiCroce, Peter Elbow, Beverly Fatherree, Lloyd Flanigan, Russ Hart, Cliff Haury, Roger Garrison, Rich Gossweiler, Pryor Hale, Tom Hyder, Jill Karle, Mary Jane King, Harold Kolb, Frank Lovelock, Ken Macrorie, Donald Murray, Raymond Nelson, Charles Nilon, Bill Owen, Jewell-Ann Parton, Nell Ann Pickett, Steve Railton, Mark Reynolds, Mary Wescott Riser, George Smith, Louise Zandberg Smith, Tamyra Turner, George Vaughan, Jane Walpole, Bettye Walsh, Bill Wood, and scores of other writers, scholars, and teachers who continue to guide me.

To Jnanam MacIsaac for inspiration and generous assistance with the manuscript. To Maj-Britt for the spirit of beginning. To Joyce Broderick, Michael Farruggio, Linda Johnson, Max Katx, Cheryl Lewis, Maj-Britt, and Randall Nordstrom for allowing me to include your work. Also to Donna Kelly and other students for your willing contributions.

To my sons Richard and Erik, my stepsons Gordon and Jay, and my stepdaughter Magnolia for being who you are and teaching me what matters.

Especially to my wife Victoria P. Young for your bountiful love and support; insightful, tough-minded reading; and savvy coaching of your sometimes-resistant husband. For our music, too.

Dick Harrington
July 1997

For Brick and Lenore

Contents

1

Collaboration

2

Roles

3

The First Group Session

4

Audience and Voice

5
Exploring

6
Drafting
Composing Your Working Draft

7

Drafting

Learning to Respond at the Drafting Stage

8

Drafting

Sample Student Responses

9
Drafting
Presenting and Responding at the Drafting Stage

10
Smoothing Ruffled Feathers

11
Refining
Learning to Refine Style

12

Proofing

Learning to Detect Annoyances

13
Odds and Ends

1

Collaboration

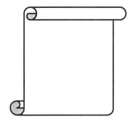

Inviting Collaboration

Welcome to college composition. You walk into the classroom, sit down in a cluster of strangers, and wonder what your professor and the course will be like. The professor stands and talks not only about course requirements but also about working together in small groups. You look around at the strange characters, hoping you won't get stuck working with that gray-haired woman in jeans next to you or that stiff-looking guy over there with horn-rimmed glasses and a necktie. Perhaps you feel insecure about your writing and dread the idea of showing it to anyone. Or perhaps you're confident about your writing and question why you need college composition at all.

For most students, learning to write at college level is a big step, often bigger than they expect. But it's manageable. It takes intention, daily work, coaching from a good teacher, and informed collaboration with a few trusted readers. This little book is a guide to such collaboration. It's also a guide to work that teachers expect of students on their own. I invite you to read it and turn to it as a handbook, a companion to the other tools selected to help you. I've composed it with you in mind, and I invite you to believe in the power of these tools to foster success and satisfaction in the work of college writing.

Only in the last thirty years or so have teachers of college writing begun to understand the value of collaboration. We've begun to notice our own habits as writers as well as the habits of other professionals. In doing so, we've learned two essential things about ourselves. We revise a lot. And we have special people who

serve as allies in revision. Whether family members or friends, colleagues or professional editors, special people read our writing and respond in ways that inform our
revision process.

My wife Victoria is such an ally. She reports honestly how my writing occurs
for her, showing me where it's clear or confusing, complete or inadequate, compelling or ordinary. When I allow my feelings to get hurt, she also coaches me not to
take her remarks personally and to get on with the job of revision. In this course you
learn to collaborate primarily with your instructor and your writing group, which
includes you and, preferably, three classmates. Your instructor will clarify whether
you might collaborate with others as well.

By introducing collaboration and revision into our classrooms, we've brought
about a revolution in the teaching and learning of writing. More than ever before in
the history of education, our students can now learn methods for producing good
writing in school, work, and personal life. If you're already a good writer, you can
make yourself better. Students who've learned to collaborate—and bring about significant revision—often speak of it as some of their most memorable learning. Your
instructor and I want you to experience the excitement and satisfaction of working
with others and producing better writing than you ever believed possible.

Writing Is Doing

Learning to write is more like learning to play tennis or fiddle music than like
learning college history, for example. In college history you mostly study information and ideas that have been gathered and interpreted by experts, including your
professor. In most undergraduate courses you're not expected to locate primary
sources and draw original conclusions. Although you're expected to think insightfully, you're not expected to conduct yourself as an historian, in other words. Learning to write is different. It's a craft—an act—that you learn mainly by engaging in it.
Instead of spending much class time learning about writing in the abstract, you
spend much of each class period working on actual writing in progress—your own
writing and the writing of your peers. You master specific roles, tasks, and relationships that enable you to produce good writing in various situations and help others
produce good writing, too.

You learn by ongoing involvement to anticipate what may create your intended
effect on intended readers. It used to be that a student writer's only reader was the
teacher, who responded mainly as a judge after the writing was completed. Collaboration provides you with various readers during the writing process, including the
instructor and your writing group. In experiencing their different responses, you
develop a feel for effective rewriting of the current piece and of future pieces. You
also develop the vocabulary and ability to discuss writing. Much of the learning
happens in the interactive process of experiencing various responses to your writing
and to the writing of your peers. Your instructor coaches—teaching, inspiring, reading with a professional eye, evaluating, guiding.

Assuming Responsibility

It may take some adjustment in your thinking to understand and accept the responsibilities expected. College composition is usually a required course, not one you choose. Yet to bring about progress in learning to write, you make a big commitment of time, effort, and openness to growth. You take responsibility for making things happen in your writing and in your group.

The challenging process of writing is both a social act and a solitary act. It's social in that its purpose is usually to communicate with others. It's also social in that others can help you learn to communicate with the intended impact. It's solitary in that it requires the act of sitting down alone and working hard at writing and rewriting to bring about such communication. Collaboration works only if everyone completes the solitary work required. Let's say your writing group is scheduled to respond to each member's working draft on Wednesday. The session will succeed only if each member has spent enough time writing and rewriting to produce a good working draft.

How much time is enough? That will vary from person to person and assignment to assignment. It's not unusual for a student writer to spend four or five hours or more of brainstorming, fastwriting, drafting, and redrafting to produce a working draft of a 500-word essay, before seeking formal responses from the instructor and/or the writing group. Also, before seeking responses, you study your draft systematically, with certain questions in mind: What have I tried to accomplish? How well have I accomplished it? What must I do to improve it? (These particular questions come from one of my favorite teachers of writing, Donald Murray.)

Thinking about these questions helps prepare you intellectually for the responses of others, whether or not they experience your draft in the same way(s) you do. Having studied your draft systematically beforehand helps you know what you've written and aids in the discussion with your instructor and/or group. It's necessary to prepare yourself emotionally for constructive criticism. Expect to revise further. Look forward to seeing your draft with new eyes. Enter each session with determination not to feel or act defensive. Open yourself to all responses, whether you agree or not. Oftentimes, the responses I most want to reject when I first hear them turn out to be the most valuable in my revision process.

You also prepare yourself to shift roles and become a responsible reader of the drafts of others. You open yourself to the subject matter and the style of writing. You take seriously each piece of writing and do your part in aiding each group member's process of revision. You serve as an ally, whether or not you feel like it that day. It's your job. And your group will appreciate your involvement and contribution.

Writing in Stages That Fit You

I remember hearing Donald Murray, winner of a Pulitzer Prize for editorial writing, say years ago that the writing process is a plate of spaghetti. Thoughts, feelings, words, the processes of getting writing onto paper seem mixed all up together. Writers begin with some purpose in mind, but as they write, too many ideas and avenues open up. They feel confused, lost in a tangle of streets and intersections. Worse perhaps, some writers, reluctant to write down their jumbled thoughts, stare paralyzed at the blank page or computer screen. For many writers in the early stages of composing a piece, the paragraphs and pages feel inadequate or jumbled or derailed. Murray's plate-of-spaghetti metaphor describes, in other words, both the writer's mind in a state of confusion and the early writing in a state of jumble.

Yet, whatever their problems, successful writers discover methods that help untangle their thoughts and produce a readable text. They learn that the processes of composing involve a series of unpredictable tanglings and untanglings. They learn to anticipate, accept, and address the tangles, though for most writers the process may continue to appear and feel much like spaghetti. A given writer begins to notice, for instance, that no matter how hard s/he tries to make the writing perfect the first time through, s/he always has to rewrite extensively later. So, writers build into the writing schedule time to rewrite, and write more quickly at first instead of wasting time trying to perfect what is not ready to be perfected. Most writers end up composing in stages of some sort, individually tailored. Because different people approach writing in different ways, it's not accurate to identify particular steps or even generic steps that all writers use. Still, its useful for teaching and learning to define and use broad stages in the production of writing, stages that are based on numerous studies of professional writers and that each student can tailor to his or her own quirks.

EXPLORING DRAFTING REFINING PROOFING

I encourage students to observe their own attitudes and habits regarding writing, to decide consciously what works and what doesn't, and to try out new methods that might bring improvement in the overall process and writing produced. The stages offer a four-part frame for self-examination and for adopting new practices.

In writing this book, I wanted to show graphically how a writer developing a piece transforms it—and perhaps his or her own state of mind—from Murray's plate of spaghetti to whatever metaphor might depict a finished piece and a clearer head. I started drawing with my computer and ended up making the first stage, EXPLORING, look like this

the second stage, DRAFTING, like this

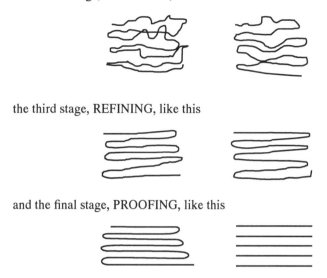

the third stage, REFINING, like this

and the final stage, PROOFING, like this

Writing involves highly complex activities of body and mind. It's so complex that even accomplished writers bog down when they try to perform all activities at once. But it's especially difficult for developing writers. I've watched second-graders trying to create a story, attend to sentence structure, and spell the words correctly at the same time. It's painful to see. Preoccupation with sentence structure and spelling impedes the creative process. A good second-grade teacher coaches students to complete the story in stages: first, to explore possibilities; second, to compose the story freely; third, to choose some better words and smooth out the sentences; and fourth, to correct the spelling and other mechanics. Obviously, something of each stage goes on at every stage. But working in stages allows concentrated effort on certain dimensions of writing—and not others—at a given time. It's important for the students to practice writing in stages, in the interest of improving their ways, and it's also crucial for the teacher to recognize and accept ways that students successfully tailor methods to their own personalities and habits. A college student may try, for instance, to draft an essay without having done enough reading, notemaking, and other exploring of the subject. The teacher might logically suggest more work in the exploring stage. Then the student might turn around and explain that s/he always starts out trying to draft to discover what s/he knows and doesn't know. The student has discovered a method of exploring that looks like drafting and works well for calling up information and ideas.

In EXPLORING, generally, you put your mind to the largest elements: strategies for reading, thinking, and writing; topic; intention or focus; voice; audience; and promising information and ideas. You write much more than you'll need to ensure an array of good material.

CONCERNS
Strategies for Exploring

WRITER
Develop strategies for
  reading, thinking, writing
Gather information and ideas
Make notes
Explore by writing

Topic
Intention (Focus)
Voice (Persona)
Audience
Information
Ideas

In DRAFTING, you consider further these same large elements, though perhaps with a clearer sense of direction, and you compose an appropriate working draft, given your intention and audience. Trying to focus on one main purpose, you select and arrange the best appropriate material from your exploratory writing. In the process, you probably discover new insights as well. As necessary, you seek better strategies for the act of drafting. A good working draft may still be rough when it arrives for the first scheduled session at this stage, but it shows signs of thoughtful rewriting toward a successful finished piece.

CONCERNS
Strategies for Drafting
Intention (Focus)
Voice (Persona)

WRITER
Draft freely
Expect to rewrite
Redraft as needed

Audience
Selection
Arrangement
Development

In REFINING, you put your mind to finer matters of presentation: your opening, rhythm and flow of sentences, word choice and imagery, transitions, closing, format, and strategies for the act of refining. You read your draft into a tape recorder, listen back, feel the writing with your ears as well as your eyes, sense what works and what doesn't at the level of the passage, the sentence, the word. In the process, it's hard not to correct smaller surface errors you notice, such as misspelled words. But you try not to focus on proofing yet because at the moment you want to learn how to improve larger elements of style. After making whatever revisions seem appropriate, you bring your draft to the refining session.

WRITER
Refine style
Record draft on tape;
  listen back and refine
Run style-check

CONCERNS
Strategies for Refining
Opening
Rhythm and flow
Diction and imagery
Transitions
Closing
Format

In PROOFING, you develop practical methods for detecting and correcting problems in grammar, usage, punctuation, spelling, and other mechanics. You run the computer spell-check and grammar-check. You record your draft on audiotape and then, while listening back, you proof and correct on your own as best you can before bringing your draft to a proofing session.

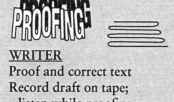

WRITER
Proof and correct text
Record draft on tape;
  listen while proofing
Run spell-check
Run grammar-check

CONCERNS
Strategies for Proofing
Grammar
Usage
Punctuation
Mechanics
Documentation
Format

Collaborating in Stages

As you might expect, these four stages provide useful openings for collaboration. Helpful collaboration, unscheduled and scheduled, can happen often during the writing process. You might phone a member of your group to get clarification about an assignment. You might talk through your ideas with a friend. You might meet your instructor during office hours for help on your first draft. I encourage any unscheduled help that doesn't involve others' doing your work for you. Because I believe so heartily in scheduled sessions, especially at the stages of drafting, refining style, and proofing, I require them as a regular part of my writing classes. As four classmates learn to work together systematically, intuitively, spontaneously, and naturally, they can develop remarkably as writers and readers as well as listeners, speakers, and thinkers. This book offers distinct, practical tested guidelines for scheduled sessions at each stage. The stages enable your writing group as well as your instructor to concentrate on certain elements—and not others—at a given time. By focusing your attention on particular elements at each stage, you learn to improve them, both now and in future writing. These stages and methods, these processes for writing and collaboration, constitute some of the most important content of the course.

Collaboration at the Exploring Stage

Collaboration at this stage supports you in producing pages of exploratory writing—in using writing as a way of thinking openly. It helps you clarify the intended audience and purpose as well as gather appropriate ideas, information, and writing strategies. It also helps you discover a particular intention that will generate a purposeful draft. Sometimes in the rush of exploratory writing, you feel a breakthrough, and you just know you're ready to draft. Other times you write and write and—well, your wheels just spin. Often, a few minutes' conversation with your group produces the breakthrough you just couldn't produce alone. If not, which sometimes happens, you can also seek professional help from your instructor. When a student says, "I'm stuck," I often ask, "What's the most important point you want to get across, and who are your intended readers?" The student's response often reveals a focus. If not, then I might point to insights I see in the exploratory writing and try to help the writer determine if one of those insights offers a meaningful focus. It's important for the writer to do as much of the talking and thinking as possible, in preparation for the solitary job of drafting.

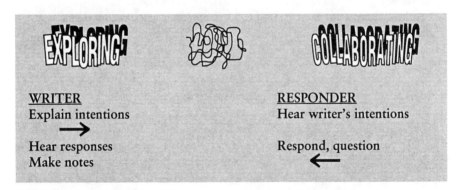

WRITER
Explain intentions
→

Hear responses
Make notes

RESPONDER
Hear writer's intentions

Respond, question
←

WRITER
Explore further as needed

Collaboration at the Drafting Stage

Here collaboration addresses larger elements of a draft—primarily main intention, audience, voice, overall arrangement, and development of thought. In the first scheduled session at this stage, you read your draft aloud to the group before giving them copies, so you and they hear it move from start to finish as a whole. They as readers respond with purpose and honesty, guided by principles and procedures that ensure constructive comments. The purpose is for the writer to experience others' responses in a way that either generates rethinking and revision of the draft or else validates the success of the piece as a good working draft. It's essential at this stage not to be distracted by matters of style and "correctness," which get plenty of attention in later stages. Also, as writers revise purposefully, they usually make refinements in smaller elements as well as larger. Why waste time helping them refine or correct elements that they might take care of themselves?

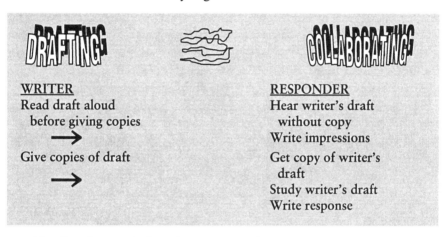

WRITER
Read draft aloud
  before giving copies
→
Give copies of draft
→

RESPONDER
Hear writer's draft
  without copy
Write impressions
Get copy of writer's
  draft
Study writer's draft
Write response

After listening to a draft read aloud and making notes of initial responses, group members each receive a copy of the draft. They study it and fastwrite a response. In the next class period, they each present an oral response, using the written response as a guide. The writer makes notes on each oral response and then collects the written responses to work from later.

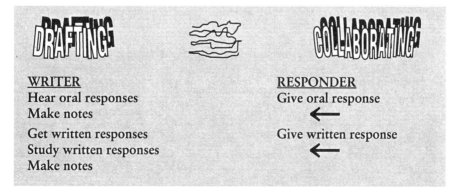

WRITER
Hear oral responses
Make notes

Get written responses
Study written responses
Make notes

RESPONDER
Give oral response
←

Give written response
←

WRITER
Draft further as needed

Collaboration at the Refining Stage

At the refining stage collaboration addresses mainly beginnings and endings, transitions, the rhythm and flow of sentences, imagery, word choice, and other elements of what we might call style. Your readers, by calling attention to passages that work and don't work so well, enable you as the writer to build on stylistic strengths and overcome weaknesses such as wordiness or blandness. You read aloud to your group, one paragraph at a time, as they read along in their copy, seeing as they listen. Note that refining style is distinguished from proofreading.

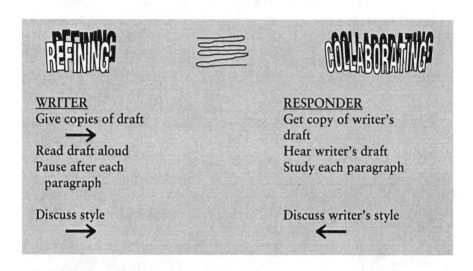

WRITER
Give copies of draft
→
Read draft aloud
Pause after each
 paragraph

Discuss style
→

RESPONDER
Get copy of writer's draft
Hear writer's draft
Study each paragraph

Discuss writer's style
←

WRITER
Refine further as needed

Collaboration at the Proofing Stage

Here collaboration addresses the writer's areas of oversight or ignorance in grammar, usage, punctuation, and mechanics as well as documentation and format. In the proofing session, you as the writer and other group members proofread together in pairs, discussing every question raised about a comma or capital letter or run-together sentence or deviance from the specified style for documentation. You become an able proofreader by learning to employ your intuitive and learned sense of language as well as your writing handbook and the coaching of your classmates and instructor. The goal is not merely to "correct" a particular paper, but also to identify and fill gaps in your ability—for the future.

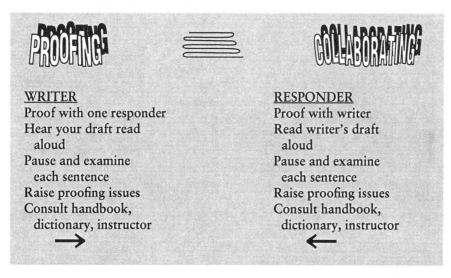

WRITER
Proof with one responder
Hear your draft read
  aloud
Pause and examine
  each sentence
Raise proofing issues
Consult handbook,
  dictionary, instructor
  →

RESPONDER
Proof with writer
Read writer's draft
  aloud
Pause and examine
  each sentence
Raise proofing issues
Consult handbook,
  dictionary, instructor
  ←

WRITER
Proof further as needed

Collaboration Beyond Proofing

Collaboration ought to continue after you finish papers and turn them in. Learn how to benefit from your instructor's professional responses, both oral and written, whether to individual papers or to the collection in your portfolio. Someone said that a piece of writing is never finished but merely abandoned. A writing course is like that. You keep on improving your abilities until the term ends.

Writing and Collaborating on Computers

Computers, too, have revolutionized writing and the teaching of writing. Whether you're a novice or expert, your writing class is an opportunity for developing and applying your computer skills. Many writers still prefer to explore and draft by hand. Some say they enjoy the physical act of writing longhand. It helps them experience a connection of language and thought with the written page. I now write mostly on a computer in my office at the college or in the study at home, which I share with my wife Victoria. She, by the way, avoids computers whenever possible. She wrote her doctoral dissertation by hand, 950 legal-size pages, which she then hired someone to type and retype as she made revisions. You may desire to do the same.

But obviously computers are here to stay, and they're quickly changing how people work. Many top-level executives, who used to dictate their correspondence to a secretary, now compose on a word processor and then have the secretary clean up and format the text for final proofing, signing, and sending. It's unusual these days to get along in virtually any career without word processing, E-mail, data storage, Internet access, and so many other common uses. Some residential colleges and universities now require students to buy a specified computer when they enroll.

Though I sit at my computer daily, often for hours at a time, I use it mainly for writing and E-mail. Occasionally, I search the Internet. I guide my college-prep students as they compose on computers. And I imagine ways to incorporate networked computers in my college composition courses. If you're a computer whiz, as many students are nowadays, you can teach me much more than I can teach you about computers. If you're a novice, you can learn in just a few hours how to enter and store your writing on disk. You can also learn to enter and store changes to your writing, without wasting time retyping the whole piece. In just a few weeks you'll probably wonder how you ever got along without this remarkable tool. Your instructor will clarify the options and requirements at your college, which may include use of the computer network for collaborating with classmates and the instructor online. The possibilities expand daily. In this book I include only brief discussions of computer use for writing and collaborating. Your instructor will present the specific applications expected for your class.

Encouragement

As with all things in life, interactions and results will vary, even if everyone tries hard. My suggestion is that you expect the best and be prepared for some days when you wish you were home in bed. Periodically evaluate your own work and the work of the group, communicate with one another, and keep trying. Much in our daily lives involves collaboration—with family, friends, colleagues, a variety of others. Here's an opportunity to learn methods that generate effective writing and promote effective relationships even outside the classroom.

HIGHLIGHTS

PLAN TO REWRITE

COMPOSE IN STAGES THAT SUIT YOU

TRY NEW METHODS

USE A TAPE RECORDER

INVITE COLLABORATION

COLLABORATE IN STAGES

USE COMPUTERS

USE HANDBOOK, DICTIONARY, OTHER TOOLS

BE RESPONSIBLE FOR YOUR OWN LEARNING

IF DISCOURAGED, SEEK GUIDANCE AND SUPPORT

2

Roles

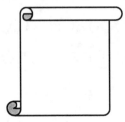

Assuming Our Roles

Let's say you're an orthopedic surgeon, and a patient is being wheeled into the operating room for arthroscopic knee surgery. An hour ago, at breakfast with your husband, you learned that he's leaving you after ten years of marriage. He and a vibrant, adventurous young woman from his aerobics class plan to buy a rafting company on the Colorado River. Your patient has every right to expect you—does he not?—to put aside your pain and outrage—to act like your normal, caring, competent, professional self. He expects you to focus purely on the arthroscope and the trimming of his torn cartilage—no matter how you feel personally. As a physician, you're committed to excellence, you've sworn the Hippocratic oath, and you do perform to the best of your ability. You even joke as usual to help the patient relax during the procedure. Your responsibility in this class is similar to the surgeon's.

Each time you enter the class, you focus your attention on the people and work at hand. As necessary, you transform yourself. It's both a privilege and a responsibility to serve in a writing group. Being human, you're bound sometimes to have feelings and thoughts that want to hold you back. Perhaps you've just learned of an illness in your family or just received a huge bill for a new clutch in your Toyota. For family crises and other emergencies, of course you may need to neglect school temporarily—or longer. But in less severe cases, you try to leave nagging matters outside the door and get on with the work. You tell your group that a personal matter is bothering you and request their understanding and help in keeping you focused. Class work goes on, and if at all possible, you do your part to make it productive.

In our daily lives we move quite naturally—and sometimes not so naturally—from role to role. Each morning when I wake up, in my role as husband I greet my wife Victoria. If I need to wake Magnolia, I do so in my role as her stepfather. I greet her differently because our relationship is different and thus my role is different. As I prepare myself for the day, I often think, in my role as teacher, about upcoming classes because I want to assume my teaching role effectively. Or I might think, in my role as musician, about the Friday night dance we're going to play for. I sometimes feel self-conscious about my fiddling, and it helps if I rehearse my role in my mind and imagine myself playing at my best.

Later, at the college I might receive a phone call, five minutes before class, from a friend who's in the midst of a personal crisis. In my role as friend, I listen supportively and arrange to talk later. On my way to class, concerned, upset, I compose myself into my role as teacher. It wouldn't be professional or right for me to allow my feelings about my friend to interfere with my students' learning. I remain the same person in these different roles, but I emphasize different parts of myself. And so it goes through our lives.

Intention and Consciousness

We develop ourselves as human beings by assuming each of our roles with greater intention and consciousness. What it takes is commitment to certain values and/or behavior that we want to assert in a particular role. As a father and stepfather, for instance, I believe nothing is more important than unconditional love. If a crisis develops with my sons or stepsons or stepdaughter, the first thing I want them to know is that I love them, no matter what, and I'm available to support them. When I feel exasperated or angry with one of them, I sometimes have to work deliberately and consciously to demonstrate that love and support. Of course, I sometimes fail. But my intention to act from my feeling of unconditional love empowers me to act from it more often—to fulfill my role as father or stepfather in the way I prefer—in the way I've chosen.

For another example, as a writing teacher I've learned that students unlock their thoughts and feelings about a subject more by talking and writing than by listening to me. In conferences during their exploratory writing, I teach them more if I ask questions and encourage them to talk than if I talk very much myself. This idea goes against what we may traditionally assume about teaching and learning. Also, I like to talk. So I struggle with myself to assume the role, in my teaching, of questioner and listener rather than talker. The more I've practiced questioning and listening, the better I've gotten at doing it.

Aligning Your Goals

Perhaps it's obvious that to succeed as a student, you establish certain goals and behaviors for each course. You have the best chance of succeeding if you align your goals and behaviors with the teacher's expectations. We college teachers have many expectations, and oftentimes we don't specify some because we assume you know and accept them. You'll perform more effectively in your writing group if you understand the values and behaviors expected and if you perform accordingly—making conscious, deliberate choices about your various roles in the class. Education is a deliberate act of personal development. When you sign up for a required math class, knowing math seems unnatural to you, you're deciding to take it on, to learn it no matter what, to shoot the rapids even if you dump the canoe and end up cold and wet holding onto an overhanging branch. Henry Thoreau went to live at Walden Pond because he wanted to "drive life into a corner" and thus learn its essential nature. You decide deliberately what you want to accomplish in the context of your teachers' expectations, and set about doing so.

Professors Develop, Too

I mentioned in the introduction that the last thirty years has brought a major breakthrough in the teaching and learning of writing. It's really two breakthroughs. Our new attention to writing as a process reveals that—especially for developing writers—the quality of writing produced often depends upon the methods of writing used to produce it. Our new attention to collaboration reveals its generative power to help improve students' methods of writing and their writing itself. It's hard to imagine a writing course without all three components—just as it's hard now to imagine writing without word processing. Teachers have always wanted their students to succeed. Our new awareness of writing as processes that students can adapt to their own individual needs and our new awareness of the possibilities of collaboration—these breakthroughs are as exciting to writing teachers as lasers have been to eye surgeons.

And so, we who teach writing have renewed ourselves professionally and adapted our methods and expectations accordingly. Successful students align their goals with the expectations of the instructor and, accordingly, create their role(s) as students. I include a list of expectations commonly held in our profession to help you align your goals with the expectations of your writing teacher.

Quality of Writing

Methods of Writing

Collaboration

Expectations
QUALITY OF WRITING

❖   Learn to compose essays/articles that are effective in content, voice, focus, arrangement, development, paragraphing, attribution, documentation, sentence construction, word choice/imagery, other matters of style, grammar, usage, punctuation, mechanics, and format.

❖ Develop comprehension of informative, thought-provoking articles and books. Summarize clearly and pointedly. Develop your own thoughts convincingly in response.

❖ Develop appreciation for effective uses of language in the writing and speaking of others and in your own writing and speaking.

❖ Develop comprehension and appreciation of imaginative literature (short story, novel, poem, play, film).

❖ Use research tools effectively, such as computer and print indexes, CD-ROM, and the Internet, to locate sources appropriate to a subject you're investigating.

❖ Make research notes systematically and efficiently, in a manner that will serve you even for large projects.

❖ Synthesize ideas and information from a variety of respectable sources.

Expectations
METHODS OF WRITING

❖ Observe your own writing methods. Determine what methods help and what methods hinder you as a writer.

❖ Honor your own writing methods that work productively for you.

❖ Use the course as an opportunity to try out and adopt more effective methods.

❖ Understand and accept that writing is a recursive process that both moves forward and yet keeps turning back on itself. Expect to rewrite and rewrite and rewrite.

❖ Allow yourself to work in stages (exploring, drafting, refining, proofing). Learn more by attending to certain things and not others at a time.

❖ Plan your time and muster the effort to keep up with coursework. Realize that in a writing course something is due nearly every class period (several pages of exploratory writing or a working draft or some other stage of a piece in progress). Expect to work two or three hours outside of class, sometimes longer, for every hour in class.

❖ Understand the essentiality of writing, reading, thinking, listening, and speaking differently for different purposes. For instance, to be a good writer, you must learn to read your own writing globally (as a whole), regionally (passage by passage), and locally (letter by letter).

❖ Use a tape recorder to help you hear and see the features of your writing.

❖ Understand and accept that personal development—in reading, writing, thinking, speaking, listening—necessarily involves challenge, determination, hard work, and discomfort. Expect self-doubt and frustration, for instance, if your instructor requires that you practice fastwriting and you're used to perfecting each sentence before going on. Open yourself to new possibilities and give them a chance.

❖ Understand and accept that writing involves every part of you—body, heart, mind, and spirit. Realize the potential for satisfaction in personal growth and self-expression.

❖ Use the computer as a tool for writing and collaboration.

Expectations
COLLABORATION

❖ Create in your group an environment of commitment, involvement, support, trust, and dependability.

❖ Discuss regularly (virtually every meeting) how the group works or needs to work as a group. Expect breakdowns and create solutions that are effective for all.

❖ Learn about and practice the craft of coachability and coaching, whether or not you're the designated leader of your group.

❖ Support the leadership of your group. When a problem develops, work through it together. If necessary, seek professional coaching from your instructor.

❖ Experience the value of learning with others. Accept coaching from your instructor and from your group—about your writing, about your writing methods, and about your work as a group member. Listen to them and write down what they say, even if you disagree at the time.

❖ Expect discomfort such as defensiveness, acknowledge it, and don't let it stop you from opening yourself to others' well-meant remarks.

❖ Follow guidelines to develop your effectiveness as a responder, as a writer, and as a group leader (if applicable). Realize it will take considerable commitment and practice. If needed, seek professional coaching from your instructor.

❖ Learn to attend to a draft (both your own and another's) in order to conceptualize it—to get it—as a whole piece of writing.

❖ Learn to make notes while reading and/or listening.

❖ Learn to provide the writer with both reader-based responses and criterion-based responses. Convey your experience of the piece of writing, what strikes you as effective, and what you want to know more about. Learn the craft of descriptive and interpretive responding rather than merely evaluative responding.

❖ After you've mastered the roles and tasks embodied in the guidelines, if you envision a more effective way than the guidelines indicate, meet with the instructor, explain your idea, and suggest that your group be supported in trying it out. Be responsible in coaching your instructor.

Inviting Coaching

People who want to realize their best—in dancing or tennis or pottery—usually get themselves a coach. We usually associate coaching with team sports, which we would hardly dream of learning to play without a coach. Who would teach fundamentals? Who would stretch the players and the team into full realization of potential? We trust the master coach to know what we must do, train us to do it, and involve us in doing it to the best of our ability. The famous pro-football coach Tom Landry said, "Coaching is when I get you to understand things you don't understand so you can do things you wouldn't otherwise do."

An excellent example is the early training scenes from the movie the *Karate Kid*. The karate master promises to train the boy in karate. The boy promises to do what he's told without question. The old man has him wash and wax several cars, sand a large wooden floor, and paint the fence and house. For each job, the master requires a particular motion of the hands. With mounting confusion, frustration, and anger, the boy threatens several times to quit. Finally, the old man reveals the many fundamentals of karate the boy has internalized unknowingly by repetition of the movements of washing, waxing, sanding, and painting. The greater lesson is trust of the coach and the coaching process.

Besides getting themselves a master coach, people who want to realize their best also put themselves in the company of others who wish to do the same. Athletes work out with teammates and engage in competition. Many musicians practice and perform with others. Potters often interact with other potters about pottery. Writing may be different from karate or tennis or pottery, but there's much to gain from adapting coaching to the teaching and learning of writing—both master coaching and peer coaching. You may be thinking, "Yeah, but what about some of the world's greatest guitar players who never had a lesson in their lives?" You've got a point. But interviews with them usually reveal that they grew up listening over and over to the playing of Django Rinehart or Jimi Hendrix or Stevie Ray Vaughan or some other world-class players. Though they have no teacher as such, they master the playing of the masters and at the same time develop their own style.

Outside of sports we usually call the coach a teacher, master, tutor, mentor, or some other. I like the term coach for writing classes. It carries less baggage than some of the other words. It works for peer relationships as well as the teacher-student relationship. And it serves well as a verb. You can say, "Will you coach me on this?" "Would you like some coaching on this?" "S/he's a very good coach." And so forth.

The Craft of Coachability

The secret of coaching is coachability—the willingness and skill to be coached. I call it a craft because, like shaping clay on a potter's wheel, coachability must be—and can be—learned. Not everyone can produce artful pottery, to be sure; but nearly everyone can learn to center and shape clay into a recognizable form. Likewise, through training and practice, nearly anyone can develop coachability. To develop it, most people need instruction and guidance from someone experienced in the coaching process. Once you develop it, though, you become open to the possibility of being coached by not only a master coach but also anyone and everyone around you. There's an old saying from the Far East: When the student is ready, the master appears. Often in life, we go along doing what we think is our best, hoping to avoid criticism. As a result, we rarely come close to imagining, much less realizing, our best.

I have a streak of independence and stubbornness that goes along with my self-consciousness. I like to do things my way and yet I often want people to accept me. As I look back over my fifty-five years, I see many instances where I'd have done much better had I made myself available for coaching. One of my tricks was to work on something by myself until I could get it right. Only then would I try it in front of others. Several years ago, in the interest of fitness, I joined a health club and began aerobics, which I enjoyed in every way—except one. I couldn't jump rope very well and I admired that ability in others. During class I'd get frustrated during the rope-jumping segments. I expended too much energy with very little grace. So, one day after class I stood alone out there on the aerobics floor, in full view of the forty-or-so people pumping iron, riding cycles, stretching, seeking to admire themselves in the huge wall mirrors. I practiced and practiced, improving but still not looking anything like the ultimate rope-jumper, a boxer working on footwork and conditioning. A woman walked over and said, "Try this rhythm," which she demonstrated. I did and it felt better. A guy walked up and said, "You're a real inspiration, man, standing out here all alone making a fool of yourself like this. I wouldn't dare, but it's the best way to learn." I laughed and kept on jumping. Soon another guy came up and showed me how he jumps. It wasn't long before I was jumping smoothly and gracefully, and inside of a week I was adding different steps and doing tricks with the rope. (If you could see me now, you might think, "He ought to sign up for that aerobics class again." You'd be right.)

Notice how in my rope-jumping example I risked feeling vulnerable and exposed as a clumsy rope jumper. Because I did, I became coachable and hence very good at jumping. Many students who haven't experienced group work in writing classes feel, understandably, self-conscious or worse when expected to bring copies of unfinished, imperfect drafts for peers to study and respond to. The process requires daring and trust. Not only can the group experience help liberate you from perpetual fears and anxieties, but it can also help support you in meeting the immense rigors of college. When I started college in the late fifties, about all that seemed to matter was the quality of writing produced. The teacher made an assignment, we did what we could to write it on our own, the teacher marked and graded it as a finished product, and we were expected to do better on the next one. There was little or no attention to how we produced the writing and how we might improve our methods in the future. Students who had written a lot in high school had usually stumbled upon methods that had worked somehow for them. Even they faced quite a challenge to meet the new rigors of college. Many students felt lost and threatened because they couldn't seem to produce what the teacher wanted. Many did poorly, either because they didn't work hard enough or because they simply didn't know how to go about writing. Collaboration with other students was virtually unthinkable. It was considered a form of cheating, an honor violation ("On my honor as a student I have neither given nor received help on this paper"). Designers of courses in college composition didn't seem to notice that "real" writers, including college professors, usually collaborate with one or more colleagues.

Rigorous Expectations

Beginning college students often feel quite jolted by the rigorous expectations of college professors. My writing classes include recent graduates from high school, working people, retirees, immigrants (some of whom are well educated in their own language), and returning students who didn't succeed at college the first time around. The median age is twenty-nine. As you can imagine, many have already experienced life as adults. Many know the demands and satisfactions of work. Still, all must adapt to the special rigors of academia. Take for instance a man in his late twenties who has worked for ten years as a carpenter. He has many skills, a family, and an established way of life. He's decided he wants a college degree and certification as an architect. He's used to hard work, eight or ten hours a day at a building site and at least three or four hours preparing meals, reading to his kids, taking them to music lessons, helping them practice and do their homework, and doing the many other things people do. But he's not accustomed to three hours a week in class, several hours in the library and on the Internet researching a topic, and several more hours writing and rewriting. He understands and accepts that

I expect a minimum of nine hours a week outside of class, but he must acquire the new set of work habits required. If he's a part-time student who is still working as a carpenter, he must add about twelve hours to his already-busy life. If he's a full-time student taking, say, five courses, he must learn to spend something like fifty hours a week just on academic work, the equivalent of his previous full-time job. Especially recent graduates of high school aren't normally used to so many hours expected outside of class.

Besides the increased workload, college students also must adapt to the increased expectations for critical thinking. Writing is thinking. To improve the quality of your writing, you work at developing the quality of your thought. We as human beings think primarily in language. To develop the quality of your thought, you work at developing the quality of your language. A college writing instructor can fairly expect you to improve in reading, thinking, writing, listening, and speaking. These abilities—our special gifts as humans—take a whole lifetime to develop. A college education is merely a beginning. Abilities in language and thought develop best, not in isolation, but in natural contexts of reading (and viewing), writing with a purpose, and interacting with people. Your writing group offers an ideal context for such natural language development.

My expectations as a teacher are typical. I expect thoughtful reading of good literature and development of research skills in the library and on the Internet, along with a sensible method for making notes and organizing research materials. I expect papers that reveal a thorough exploration of a subject. Students focus on one main area and consider it in detail, learning the relation of fact and opinion, drawing sound conclusions. I expect clear, precise writing in a style appropriate to the writer, subject, and audience—qualities achieved usually by careful rereading and recrafting. I expect near-perfect proofreading, meticulous consideration of grammar, usage, punctuation, mechanics, format, and documentation. I expect word processing, not only for final copy but for successive drafts along the way. I expect ongoing improvement in thinking, listening, reading, writing, speaking, and interacting with people. I also expect students to develop a sophisticated ability to work together at each stage of writing.

I view my students as adults who take responsibility for their own behavior. I have a cut policy allowing a week's worth of classes to be missed without penalty. When a student who's missed that many, misses two more in a row, doesn't contact me until later, brings me after the fact a doctor's "excuse," and expects me to forgive the extra cuts unconditionally, I feel manipulated and exasperated. It's not that I'm not concerned about the student's health. I am. It's not that I'm unwilling to be flexible. I am, if the situation warrants. It's that I expect students to arrange things beforehand, and if that's impossible because of a medical emergency, I expect them to arrange ways to make up the work missed and accept the stated conditions of the course. In fact, with students who do take responsibility as adults, I'm likely not to impose a penalty for unavoidable extra cuts. Their overall pattern of behavior signifies responsibility and assures me they'll make up the work and get back on schedule with their group.

Where's the Teacher?

The powerful shift in our classrooms to the stages of writing and to collaboration creates opportunities for responsibility and coaching, much as in sports. Writing groups—and other classroom activities that further writing as an ongoing process—require students to work with one another, often independently of the instructor, much as a team plays on the court or field, while the head coach directs from the sidelines. A coach is usually not allowed on the court or field. That's because sports are supposed to be about the players playing. If you're not used to working with a writing group, you may be inclined not to trust the process or your group members. You may feel compelled, after "going through the motions" with your group, to ask the instructor for "real" help.

Because your instructor is committed to your progress and wants to help you, s/he may request that you return to your group and commit yourself to the process. If you're really stuck, then s/he may choose to work with you individually and/or to coach the group as well. Unless there's a special problem, such as a lack of commitment by group members, the group process will create remarkable possibilities for your growth as a writer—greater possibilities in most cases than working with the instructor only. For the interactive process to achieve its power, group members need to interact with belief in the group's collective potential. Allow time for such belief to flourish. Get past the common notion that the only "real" learning comes from the teacher.

Declaring Your Personal Intention

As your own barriers to real learning pop up, there's power in speaking aloud what you want to accomplish or overcome. If something is bothering you, you can probably transcend it during class by declaring your intention to do so and requesting support. If you're not a good listener, you can improve by declaring to the group your intention to listen more attentively and then allowing yourself to grow into that intention. At the start of each group session the leader will ask each member to declare a specific personal intention for that day. If you as writer acted defensive in the previous session when the group responded to your paper, for this session you might declare your intention to accept responses more generously. You might also invite the leader and the advocate to coach you if you do act defensive. The point is that by taking responsibility for your own behavior, you increase your chances of overcoming whatever goblins stand in your way. We all have goblins—fear of exposure, fear of failure, laziness of mind, arrogance, elitism, racism, sexism, agism, ethnocentrism, social insecurity, a voice from the past saying "not good enough," whatever. One purpose of education is to understand ourselves and others.

Leader

Advocate

Writer

Responder

Leader

In your group there are four main roles to be established and refined: leader, advocate, writer, and responder. The leader orchestrates each session, including the solving of problems, keeps the group focused on the work, collects and distributes materials, and communicates with the professor about group matters. If a member speaks in a nonconstructive manner, the leader intervenes and redirects the member's line of speaking. If a member speaks longer than the specified time, the leader intervenes to ensure equitable coverage of all drafts. The best writing groups usually include natural chitchat and joking along the way, interwoven with systematic work. The leader ensures a healthy balance. It's a demanding job, being the heavy, but it's essential and offers good experience for the leader as well as the group. Ideally, group members coach the leader—diplomatically—in becoming more effective.

LEADER

Open each session. Lead discussion of the group's intentions and procedures.

Observe the group in action.

Coach members who stray from guidelines or from the job at hand.

Serve as mediator. Coach the group when breakdowns occur.

Represent the group in working with the instructor. When necessary, request the instructor's coaching for the group.

Collect and distribute handouts.

If a member is absent, make sure arrangements are being made to keep up the group's integrity and progress.

At the end of each session, lead the group's discussion of how the session went for each member.

Be available to coach by phone.

Advocate

The advocate's job is to support the other group members as they play out their roles. If a writer acts defensive while a responder is speaking, the advocate serves as a diplomat, intervening constructively between the two parties and negotiating a peace. Perhaps the responder's tone seems harsh and may be contributing to the writer's defensiveness. While the leader requests that the responder speak with a softer tone, the advocate encourages the writer to listen openly and not take the responder's comments personally. Perhaps the responder's message is fine, but it's hitting at something the writer needs to face. The advocate, as in the other example, encourages the writer to listen openly and not take the responder's comments as a personal attack. Or if the writer should speak harshly to the responder, the leader intervenes with the writer, and the advocate encourages the responder not to get hooked by the remark.

ADVOCATE

Support the writer if s/he appears defensive or otherwise uncomfortable during a response, especially if the responder has strayed from guidelines.

Support the responder if s/he appears defensive or otherwise uncomfortable during an interchange, especially if the writer has strayed from guidelines.

Writer

The writer's job is to present the working draft as directed by the guidelines for that particular stage and to receive responses openly to bring about thoughtful revision. *Revision* means literally to "see again," to "reconsider," to "rethink." In a group session the writer "sees" not only with his or her own eyes but also with the eyes of each responder. Being open to a variety of insights is essential for the process to work. During oral responses the writer listens intently and makes notes on virtually everything said—for later consideration. I've often found—and you'll hear me say more than once in this book—that if I feel defensive about a response to a passage of my writing, very likely that's a passage I'm going to want or need to revise later, after I've let myself accept the insight of the responder's point. Defensiveness often is a cover for a lack of security. In any case, the writer absorbs each responder's comments like a sponge soaking up spilled coffee—which may be how it feels sometimes. But after thoughtful reconsideration, accepting and rejecting various comments to suit the writer's ultimate purpose, the idea is to brew a fresh, savory pot.

WRITER

Present the writing according to guidelines, without apologies.

Receive responses and coaching in the spirit of learning.

During each oral response, listen and make notes extensively.

Talk very little. Don't defend the writing.

Redraft, or refine, or proof as necessary.

Responder

The responder in some ways has the hardest job of all—to provide comments that generate in the writer both the desire and means to revise purposefully. Much of this book and an essential piece of the writing course involve learning how to provide such responses. Most of us have developed habits of responding that don't serve a writer very well. We tend to make sweeping, judgmental comments, as our past teachers have mostly done, such as "Good paper!" or "Your idea may be good, but the paper's disorganized." Or we call attention to errors in grammar, usage, and such, without addressing the intended message and its presentation. Over the years I've learned that the most helpful comments are not evaluative but rather descriptive and interpretive. The responder helps the writer see what is actually there in the piece of writing and what actually takes place in the responder's head and heart while reading the piece. Such specific information delivered in specific terms by each responder offers the writer either a pallet of insights that generate purposeful revision or a clear validation that the piece already works as intended.

RESPONDER

Respond according to guidelines for each stage. When you or someone you're interacting with strays from guidelines, accept coaching, and move on.

Learn to grasp the writer's intention and to help the writer accomplish it, whether or not you concur. Likewise, learn to grasp the writer's budding style and to help the writer develop and refine it. In proofing, learn to help the writer detect and solve proofing issues.

Remember that virtually everything you do as a responder develops your abilities in language and thought and helps to make you a better writer as well as a better reader, listener, and speaker.

So You're Not an Expert

The shift in focus from teacher to student may startle you at first. You may wonder how four relatively inexperienced writers can help one another as much as my claims suggest. What about the teacher's expertise in language and writing? I assure you, there'll be many ways that the teacher's expertise comes into play. I also assure you, there's no need for you or your group to be experts for the group process to work its power. Your instructor and I are committed to teaching you methods of working together that require—not professional expertise—but honesty and attentiveness in listening, reading, thinking, speaking, and writing. Working together on writing immerses you—systematically, spontaneously, and simultaneously—in developing virtually all of your abilities in language.

HIGHLIGHTS

ALIGN YOUR GOALS WITH YOUR INSTRUCTOR'S EXPECTATIONS

COMMIT TO IMPROVING YOUR WRITING, YOUR METHODS OF WRITING, AND YOUR WORK WITH OTHERS

UNDERSTAND AND ASSUME THE VARIOUS ROLES REQUIRED OF YOU

TAKE RESPONSIBILITY FOR YOUR OWN BEHAVIOR

CREATE MUTUAL TRUST, SUPPORT, INTEGRITY, AND DEPENDABILITY

LEARN COACHABILITY. INVITE COACHING FROM YOUR GROUP AND YOUR INSTRUCTOR

TRUST THE GROUP PROCESS

3

The First Group Session

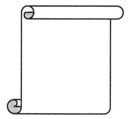

Why Four?

Three make a puny mix of personalities. Five are a crowd that can't usually finish in a class period. So, a writing group consists ideally of four classmates who are determined and trained to help one another develop as writers. From the outset it's essential to accept the responsibility of being a group member, to grasp the importance of your being prepared and present for each scheduled session (with reasonable exceptions).

How should groups be formed? Hair length? Age? Writing experience? Clothes? The evidence is mixed. It doesn't seem to matter. I've seen the most unlikely collection of people celebrate their differences and accomplish wonders together. What does matter is commitment. Four people with intention to help one another develop as writers will almost surely help one another develop as writers.

When starting a new class, I arrange the tables to accommodate groups and usually allow people to form their own. I've also used a lottery system. Follow your instructor's directions and meet your new group. It may seem like a motley crew, but things aren't always as they seem. In just a few weeks, I wager, you'll value them as allies, perhaps even as friends. A few weeks ago at a student's wedding, I was touched to visit with members of his writing group. Remember, too, that often in your life, especially on the job, you're bound to work with teams of various people. Seek possibilities unavailable to you alone.

FIRST GROUP SESSION

Arrange seating so you face one another and can hear.

Request help with special needs such as space for a wheelchair.

Introduce yourselves. Say briefly what you'd like the group to know about you.

Exchange phone numbers, addresses, and schedules.

Engage in an activity designed to help you work productively together.

Select your leader.

Select your advocate.

Select coaching partners.

Configurations

Place your desks in a tight circle of four, or sit around a table. Position yourselves as far from other groups as possible to minimize noise distraction. Perhaps your group will have its own small room or alcove. If you're meeting in an electronic writing classroom, your computers and tabletops may already be clustered. In fact, your course may involve "talking" to one another via networked computers. The writer's draft is displayed on all four screens at once. Using his or her own keyboard, a responder can write a response that appears on all four screens. Also, a responder or the writer can actually revise the writer's text. (As I discuss elsewhere, I prefer that the writer make all actual changes to be made.) Whatever the case, learn to make the best use of your surroundings. If the room is noisy, lean in close and listen more intently. Request any special arrangements you need because of a wheelchair or hearing problem. Help your group do whatever seems necessary for success.

Getting Started Working Together

For your motley collection to become a writing group, you need to get to know one another and develop trust. Start by chatting informally. Introduce yourselves and tell some things you'd like the others to know. Your instructor may have a special way for you to go about this, such as a special mission for you to accomplish

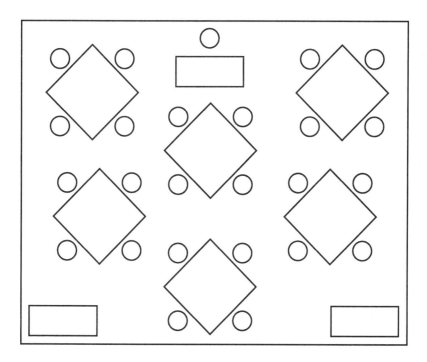

together. One I like involves learning how to read and respond to a piece of writing in four ways that become essential a few days later in the course. (I learned it from Joe Strzepek.) I hand out a short poem and assign each group one of four tasks: (1) Perform the poem. (2) Describe the poem without interpretation or evaluation. (3) Interpret the poem. (4) Evaluate the poem. Each group has twenty minutes or so to prepare its part, one member being the designated note-taker. I usually encourage the group(s) that will perform the poem to prepare outside the room.

The performing group performs the poem for the class, usually by reading it aloud and perhaps acting it out. I encourage imagination. Then the note-maker for each group reports the group's findings. The describing group(s) has the difficult task of observing and reporting only "facts" of the poem, name of the author, title, number of lines, number of stanzas, inclusion of particular words, and so forth. It's difficult simply to describe a poem as an "object" or "artifact" because we're so accustomed to interpreting as we read. The goal here, in the words of Joe Friday on the old TV detective show *Dragnet*, is "Just the facts, ma'am. Just the facts." The interpreting group(s) observes and reflects upon "meaning," upon the various interpretations that seem credible, the speaker's apparent intention(s), implied audience, feelings evoked, and the like. The evaluating group(s) decides the quality of the poem as a poem, which requires discussion of possible standards that might be applied. What makes a poem good or bad? Such group activity fosters common purpose, cohesiveness, and familiarity (as well as preparation for the types of reading and thinking required later).

Phone Numbers, Addresses, Schedules

Exchange phone numbers, addresses, and schedules, so you can reach one another if necessary. When a group member needs to miss a session, s/he'll want to arrange with the others to catch up, perhaps in a special meeting of the group. Also, plan to guide and support one another through the course, with phone calls and, if necessary, meetings outside of class. When you're struggling with, say, procrastination, what a difference it can make to talk with a classmate who also experiences the challenges of the course.

Coaching Partners

A good way to support one another is to cultivate specific partnerships of two within your group. Each student then has one particular ally for mutual coaching and for communicating with the group when an emergency pops up. I recall working on a group project that required, by mutual agreement, two scheduled coaching calls per week. The point of the call was to ask how the other was doing with the project and to discuss any problems. I found myself welcoming each call because it supported me in the work and helped to motivate me to keep active in it. Writing raises many human issues. Two scheduled coaching calls in addition to class meetings can help each student writer face the music. This partnership is a professional arrangement, not a friendship, so you needn't "like" your partner, although it can help if you do.

Leader and Advocate

Select a group leader—to help keep the work going, serve as mediator, and communicate with your instructor. Things fall apart sometimes. A designated leader can be invaluable in helping pull them back together. Also select an advocate to work in tandem with the leader, supporting a temporary victim of breached guidelines. (Both roles are described in Chapter 2.)

HIGHLIGHTS

GET TO KNOW YOUR GROUP

SEEK HELP FOR SPECIAL NEEDS

ARRANGE LOGISTICS

ALIGN YOUR GOALS WITH YOUR INSTRUCTOR'S
EXPECTATIONS

COMMIT TO IMPROVING YOUR WRITING
YOUR METHODS OF WRITING
YOUR WORK WITH OTHERS

CREATE MUTUAL TRUST, SUPPORT, INTEGRITY

LEARN TO ACCEPT COACHING FROM YOUR
GROUP AND INSTRUCTOR

TRUST THE GROUP PROCESS

4

Audience and Voice

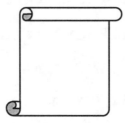

Intention, Interaction, and Audience

In your writing group you learn to develop yourself in two main roles—reader/responder and writer. Doing so teaches you about the nature of writing and reading. Both are complex interactive processes. Writing is an imagined interactive process between writer and reader via the writer's text. In the other direction, reading is an imagined interactive process between reader and writer. Understanding and building upon these two concepts can make you a better writer and a better reader. Learning to write and read takes a lifetime. At fifty-five I'm better at both than I was at forty.

The writer, wishing to convey a particular intention, imagines a certain reader or group of readers, and composes with that audience in mind. In other words, the writer imagines an ongoing interaction with the intended audience and makes linguistic choices accordingly. The reader, wishing to grasp the particular intention of a piece of writing, imagines the writer's voice and sometimes even the writer's person speaking the text. In other words, the reader, too, imagines an ongoing interaction. It may not always be the author as such speaking but rather a character—such as the narrator of a novel—whose voice was created by the author and whose voice must be recreated in the reader's mind and imagination.

WRITING AND READING:
IMAGINED INTERACTION OF WRITER AND READER
VIA THE WRITER'S TEXT

WRITER ————————▶ ◀———————— READER
CREATES   RECREATES
TEXT   TEXT

WRITER'S TEXT

We often speak of the writer's intention, and we should speak more often of the reader's intention. Why do we read? The answer is complex because we read for different purposes at different times. If we want mainly to be entertained, we might read tales of mystery or science fiction or adventure or romance. If we want mainly to be informed, we might read a grocery list, a newspaper, a weekly news magazine, a chemistry textbook, or a history of settlement in the Shenandoah Valley. If we wish to be inspired emotionally or spiritually, we might read the journal of a thinker whom we admire, or a selection of poetry, or a religious text such as the *Koran*. The ancient Greek poet Horace asserted that the purpose of good writing is "to delight and instruct." In conversation with us, were he alive, he would probably agree that the purpose of good reading is to be delighted and instructed. We usually read in order to transform ourselves—to experience being transformed by entertainment or knowledge or inspiration. Some writing achieves all three.

As your readers begin to read your writing, they aren't yet transformed. They bring to the reading process certain values and expectations, some of which you as the writer try to anticipate. But much of what happens during the reading process depends upon the capability of the writing to transform readers as they read. Another way of putting this is to say that you as the writer, in effect, create your own audience. The choices you make about content and language determine whether or not your readers are effectively transformed into the audience that you as writer imagine and desire.

TRANSFORMS READER
INTO RESPECTFUL AUDIENCE

WRITER'S TEXT

For this interaction to take place successfully, you needn't merely write what you think others may want to hear. Quite the opposite. You communicate what you feel moved to communicate, given the circumstances, in a manner that engages readers and transforms them into readers who experience being entertained or informed or inspired by the character of your writing.

Your purpose or intention in writing is to bring about such transformation in your readers. It's essential to know as much as possible about their values and expectations and to be sensitive to them as people, but more important in reaching them—and in transforming them—is writing in such a way that you attract and keep them as you convey your message. In effect, your intention is to create them as you want them to be.

Let's say you believe physicians should be required to assist terminal patients in committing suicide, if the patients have so chosen, rather than suffering long and painful deaths. You know that such practice is currently illegal and violates the medical oath to maintain life. You want to write a letter to the editor of your local newspaper that will persuade readers to take seriously the idea of doctor-assisted suicide, and you want to inspire the general assembly of your state to pass legislation approving the process. You know that many potential readers currently disagree with you or at least have doubts about legalizing such suicide. Many may not want even to entertain the idea seriously. Your intention is to engage them and help them see the value of doctor-assisted suicide to them as individuals, to their families and friends, to society at large. It's a big order, obviously, and you're certainly not going to persuade all readers to adopt your position. But succeeding with all readers is not the point, is it? You're moved to write these letters, and you want to write them so effectively that they potentially engage, inform, and inspire all readers, whether or not they actually adopt your position. Your intention is to transform them into an audience that respects your position, a position that probably feels threatening. You imagine yourself talking with them, and as you do, you hear yourself speaking in a voice—a tone—that is sensitive to their probable attitudes and feelings about suicide.

By adopting a respectful voice, you heighten your chances of their listening respectfully. No one likes to be hammered by another's point of view as though it were truth itself. To communicate successfully, you create a *persona* that speaks your heartfelt, well-considered views on the topic so sensitively and thoughtfully that your readers feel moved to interact with you. We often use the word *persona* to describe the voice speaking a poem or novel. We should use it more often for nonfiction prose as well—articles, editorials, essays, reports, and other such writing—because a nonfiction-prose writer, just as a poet or novelist, does in fact create a *persona* who presents the piece. The same writer in one piece might sound humorous, in another piece sympathetic, and in yet another piece sarcastic. We're complex personalities with many dimensions. It doesn't work to write always in the same voice. A writer searches for just the right voice from within for a certain purpose and a certain audience.

The Writer's Audience Is Always a Fiction

Still, no matter who is your intended audience, as Walter Ong revealed decades ago, you can never know surely how that person or group will react. Think about it. Imagine you've gotten yourself into a troubling situation and you need to talk it over honestly with your closest friend, someone you can always trust. As you're explaining your problem, suddenly your friend gets upset with you for what you've done and threatens to break off your relationship. S/he feels threatened and projects that feeling into your relationship. If you'd thought more about your friend's character and experiences, perhaps you might have anticipated that reaction and presented the situation differently, but in human interactions, you nearly always risk being understood in ways you don't intend. Ong's point regarding the writer's audience is that, even when writing to someone sitting in the same room with you, you can only imagine how that person will receive your message. The better you know your intended reader(s), the better chance you have of succeeding, but there are no certainties about human responses. Writing about things that matter often means taking risks, risks that you minimize by learning and developing your role as a writer and as a reader of your own writing.

Writing for Yourself

Even when writing just for yourself, as in a personal journal, there are two distinct roles involved—you as writer and you as intended reader. When writing a grocery list, says Gene Montague, the part of you that remembers writes to the part of you that forgets. Ever since I first came across his little gem many years ago, I've used it as a reminder. When writing a grocery list, I imagine various meals, snacks, and household functions and the items we need for each. If I'm planning to make black beans and rice, for which I follow my own recipe in my head, I imagine myself preparing the dish, visualizing each item I'll need: beans, garlic, cumin, salt, pepper, Tabasco, onion, green pepper, red pepper, carrot, and brown rice. Then I check to see what items we have and don't have in the cupboards, pantry, and fridge. After I've made up a shopping list, I'll usually think of something else I want or need to add. I know—and I let Montague remind me—that no matter how vivid the item appears in my mind right then, I'll nearly always forget about it in the store—unless I add it to the list.

Notice how even writing such a shopping list involves the primary dimensions of the writing process: writer's role, intended audience, and purpose. The purpose is to transform the reader—the part of me that will probably forget—into a shopper who brings home the brown rice as well as the red pepper and garlic. If the writing is successful, then it brings about the intended purpose with the intended audience. Notice, too, that the writer actually adopts two distinct roles during the writing process—the role of writer as such and the role of intended reader.

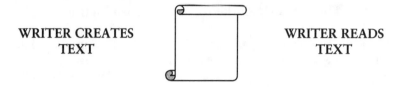

WRITER CREATES TEXT

WRITER READS TEXT

After I've written a shopping list, I read it to make sure it contains the items we need. To do so, I adopt the role of reader, which in this case derives from the role of cook or diner. That is, as reader of the list, I must imagine the items we'll need or want to cook with and/or to eat, so that I can add to the list any item left off.

Writing in a personal journal also involves the three primary dimensions of writing—writer's role, intended audience, and purpose—even when you're writing for yourself alone. What is your purpose? Last May, Victoria and I spent three weeks vacationing and performing old-time Appalachian music in France. Since I'd never been out of the U.S. before, I decided to write about our travels and adventures in a journal. I wanted to record my thoughts and feelings as well as events. In reading it over this morning, looking for a passage I might include here as an example, I realize how little space I gave to reflection on my thoughts and feelings. Busking, performing on the street, which I'd never done before, brought up lots of thoughts and feelings for me. Many villages in France have, instead of a supermarket, a designated market day each week when farmers and vendors come from far and wide to sell their goods to the local citizenry. It's common on market day to see French buskers entertaining people as they shop and socialize, and Victoria and I wanted to busk, too. Well, I sort of wanted to. The idea embarrassed me and made me anxious. Here's a brief excerpt regarding a busking experience, not on market day, while visiting our friends June and Bernard, who live high in the French Alps near Chamonix:

> *We said goodbye to Bernard at the bottom of the breathtaking tramway ride down from Mont Blanc, since he had a meeting to attend, and then we prepared to busk. I was anxious and mean-spirited, feeling I didn't really want to, but I was willing to go along because Victoria really wanted to. There was no market, just locals and tourists, and it didn't feel right to me. We parked, set up on a sidewalk, and began. There was little response—different from our previous experiences—and it was loud periodically from cars going by. June sat across the narrow street with her dog Pasco as our audience. So after a few songs, we moved on to a better place, the square near two cafes and the Casino. We got a few interested listeners, a mom and two kids, a cute boy on his bike, and some drunken teenagers who really wanted rock and roll but who gave us some money anyway. We sold no CD's or tapes and soon decided to quit—perhaps better for the experience but I'm not sure. It's definitely good for the ego to experience virtually no response. Or is it? We joked about it with June saying she enjoyed it immensely and she couldn't believe how people are, so to speak. She took photos of the happy buskers.*

The intended audience for my journal entries is the part of me that will probably forget the details of our experience and also the part of me that wants to understand myself and develop myself by reflecting on my experience. The most interesting emotions for me to explore are (1) my anxiety in anticipation of busking, (2) my apparent resentment of Victoria for persuading me to do so in the face of my anxiety, and (3) my sheer joy at having done it. In rereading the passage, I feel dissatisfied that I didn't explore those feelings in depth—especially since, in retrospect, I'm happy I agreed to busk there. I enjoy looking at the photos June took of us singing there on the street in Chamonix. One of them now hangs on our refrigerator.

I present this example to illustrate the interaction of roles in the writing process even when there is no other audience intended than the self. Obviously, in most of the writing we do, there's an intended reader beyond ourselves. But the process of composing is often similar no matter what the audience or purpose. Within those of us who write—pretty much all educated humans—there's a self that desires to be satisfied by the writing. The standards set by that self are the projection of some ideal reader that lives within us more than out there in the world. We write something, and then we shift into the role of that imagined ideal reader and read it to determine whether its voice and other characteristics meet the expected standards. If not, we rewrite and again read it to see if it's come closer to the mark. (Donald Murray calls this self "the writer's first reader.")

WRITER CREATES
TEXT

WRITER READS
TEXT IN ROLE OF
IMAGINED IDEAL
READER

NOTE: WHEN READING AND RESPONDING TO OTHERS' DRAFTS, YOU'RE LEARNING TO READ AND RESPOND TO YOUR OWN DRAFTS. YOU'RE LEARNING TO BE YOUR OWN FIRST READER.

If I could go back to our hotel room in France where I wrote that journal entry, I'd add more descriptive details about each busking experience, because it was such a grand and unusual adventure for me—so out of character. Isn't it odd thinking of a college professor playing and singing for money on the streets of a foreign village? Ernest Hemingway liked to put his characters in unusual and therefore challenging situations that tested what they were made of. For me, busking was like that in small ways, and I'd want to write a lot more about how I felt, why I resisted what turned out to be such great fun as well as quite a challenge to my ego.

Writing for Grandma

We're actually pretty experienced at adjusting our writing or speaking for different readers. Consider a middle-school girl, Diane, writing to thank her grandmother for the birthday present. She also wants to tell her about a certain boy she's met; she thinks about him a lot and sometimes feels distracted from her schoolwork, although she's a good student. Her grandmother is old-fashioned, but she loves Diane and wants to know what's going on in her life, especially now that Diane's family has moved to New Mexico. They don't get to see each other as much as when they lived in the same town back in Missouri. While writing, Diane imagines her grandmother and how she might respond to her words. The present is a sweater that she wouldn't be caught dead wearing. Still, she thanks her grandmother generously because it's, after all, the thought that counts. She feels gushy about the boy, but she knows somehow that if she expresses how she really feels about him, her grandmother might worry that she's acting beyond her age.

> *Dear Grandma. Thanks so much for thinking of me on my birthday and sending me such a nice card and sweater. I miss you and wish we could see each other more often. I like Albuquerque. The weather is nice and my school is really great. I'm making lots of new friends. There's this boy I really like. When I'm older, I hope we can go to movies and stuff. Mom says I'm too young to date, and I think she's right. What do you think? I always liked it when we talked about things. Well, I have to do my homework now. Hope to see you soon, maybe at Thanksgiving.*
> *Love, Diane.*

Imagine how different this letter would be if she were writing to her best friend back in Missouri. She'd no doubt tell much more about the boy and her feelings. *Dear Susie. I met this boy at school and, I mean, he is really. . . .* We learn at a very young age how to communicate with a variety of people. We do so by imagining or creating them within ourselves and adjusting our voice and language to suit our relationship with them and our purpose in speaking or writing. Growing up, we gain considerable experience adapting our spoken and written language to different listeners or readers. Nonetheless, there is still much to learn about the intended readers of our adult writing and about how to transform them into the respectful readers we desire them to be, whether friends or family, teachers, prospective employers, or concerned citizens. Especially challenging for many students is learning to write for the primary reader of most college writing—the professor.

The Teacher as Audience

In school or college the teacher is often the ultimate reader of student writing. So who is the teacher as audience? In other words, what ideal reader must you as a student imagine in order to satisfy the expectations of the teacher? Much of the role is unconscious on the part of the teacher—a mix of values and behavior developed over time as a professional academic grounded in a particular discipline. As a practitioner within this discipline, your teacher wants for you to learn and practice those same values and behaviors—and they're not the same from discipline to discipline, although there's much that various disciplines share, too.

The word *discipline* refers traditionally to a set of principles and practices for advancing knowledge in a given field. The assignments given you by your teachers in history, biology, mathematics, and literature usually reflect some essential activity within the discipline. The study of literature, for example, involves—among other concerns—interpretation of primary works. As a student, you have direct access to the primary works you're studying, and your teacher can well expect you to develop your own credible interpretations of assigned works through careful reading and thought. History also depends upon primary sources for information—letters, diaries, public records, and other published documents. As a history student in college, you don't usually have access to such primary sources, and so you must depend primarily on the works of historians and learn to judge which of their accounts and interpretations of events seem the most credible. In reading your work, your teacher will consciously and unconsciously consider your awareness of the values and behaviors expected in the discipline. Hence the more you learn about the nature and workings of each discipline, the better chance you have of developing yourself effectively as a writer within that discipline.

Your teachers in content areas such as history or biology are interested primarily in your displaying how you think and what you're learning in the discipline. As readers of your writing they're essentially testing you in their field. Good students demonstrate the methods of thought and learning that scholars in the discipline expect. They also develop academic voices. A typical college biology class involves primarily lecture and demonstration by the instructor. As a practitioner in the field, the instructor is teaching and displaying information, values, and behaviors essential to the discipline. In the class itself, students usually get little opportunity to act as biologists themselves. In the lab or field, however, students are expected to conduct themselves as biologists—as practitioners in the discipline. Cutting up a frog isn't just cutting up a frog. The lab instructor expects students to approach the activity as scientists—asking certain types of questions, applying certain methods, and seeking knowledge and insight about the workings of nature. Students who think they're just supposed to find and memorize parts of the frog's anatomy will miss much of the lesson. The lab is practice for life as a biologist, whether or not you intend to major in biology. In reading your lab report, the instructor is looking, consciously and unconsciously, for signs of science—a certain manner of inquiry and thought as well as a certain way of sounding. Understanding and acting upon this point will serve you well as a student, no matter what your major.

As readers, teachers sometimes become conflicted when, for instance, personal values conflict with academic values, and they may decide, consciously or unconsciously, to respond as academics. This is, after all, academia. Let's say your American history professor often lectures with a passion for the subject that engages you and at times touches you. In researching and writing your essay on child labor, on the treatment of children in nineteenth-century sweatshops, you've developed quite a passion yourself. You're deeply touched by the appalling working conditions, physical abuse, emotional abuse, long hours, low pay—and you've infused your paper with well-founded emotion as well as substantial information. Your teacher may also be touched personally and emotionally by the issue and by your paper and yet may mark you down for presenting your findings in prose that is too emotional or too personal to pass muster as good academic history. After all, the teacher might argue that there is a difference between speaking in a lecture hall and writing a formal essay. The voices sound different. In making this distinction, your professor is preparing you in part for the rigors of academic life in upper division courses, graduate school, or professional publication. Yet if your academic voice sounds too academic, then your professor might suggest you lighten up and sound a bit more human. Frankly, it's very hard to find just the right balance of the human and the academic—and even academic taste varies from reader to reader.

So, does that leave you in the dark when writing for teachers? No. A teacher as audience is really not much less or much more predictable than audiences other than teachers. No audience is completely predictable. But you can learn to observe each of your professors in action and to distinguish between personal idiosyncrasies and generic professional behavior and expectations. You can begin to notice certain ways, for instance, that historians—as against, say, biologists—gather information, learn, think, and draw conclusions. You can learn to distinguish, too, the differences in their academic voices.

Who Are You as a Responder to the Writing of Your Peers?

As a responder to the college writing of your peers, should you try to assume the role of the professor, usually the intended audience for a college essay? Or should you simply be your best self? Or should you find some middle ground between these two extremes? The answer, of course, is complex. But the most important feature of a good response is forthrightness. You give your honest observations—albeit trained observations—as a committed reader reading. The more you learn about writing and about various academic disciplines, the more effective you'll become at responding to a variety of writing by various student writers. Perhaps above all, the more vividly and fully you can report how the writing entertains, informs, and inspires you, the better information the writer gains on which to base thoughtful rewriting.

The nature of your role(s) as responder will become more and more apparent as the book and course develop. Included in the section on collaboration at the drafting stage, Peter Elbow's distinction between "reader-based" and "criterion-based" responses is useful in finding a balance between honest personal responses and responses that consider what a teacher or other professional reader might expect. Remember, also, that in college writing the teacher's expectations aren't the only issue. Your writing can transform the teacher-as-reader, just as it can other readers, into a respectful, appreciative audience. I'm delighted and give high marks when a student paper meets requirements and instructs or persuades me in unexpected ways.

HIGHLIGHTS

WRITING IS AN INTERACTION BETWEEN WRITER AND READER VIA THE WRITER'S TEXT

IN THE OTHER DIRECTION, READING IS AN INTERACTION BETWEEN READER AND WRITER

READERS READ TO BE INFORMED, ENTERTAINED, AND/OR INSPIRED

EFFECTIVE WRITING TRANSFORMS THE READER INTO A RESPECTFUL AUDIENCE

THERE IS ALWAYS AN IMPLIED IDEAL AUDIENCE EVEN WHEN WRITING FOR YOURSELF ALONE

LEARN TO BE A GOOD FIRST READER OF YOUR OWN WRITING

UNDERSTAND THE EXPECTATIONS OF ACADEMIC READERS IN VARIOUS DISCIPLINES

IN RESPONDING TO THE ACADEMIC WRITING OF PEERS, DEVELOP BALANCE BETWEEN YOUR OWN HONEST RESPONSES AND IMAGINED EXPECTATIONS OF PROFESSORS

5

Exploring

Seeking a Northwest Passage

Thomas Jefferson—and many others in the early 1800s—envisioned a navigable inland water route across the continent. The Mississippi already connected the Ohio River in the northeast and the Gulf of Mexico in the south at New Orleans. But from St. Louis northwest up the Missouri River, exploration had extended only so far. And now that the U.S. had acquired the Northwest Territory with the Louisiana Purchase, the new holdings needed to be explored and claimed from St. Louis up the Missouri into unknown territory, across the Continental Divide, and down the Columbia River to the Pacific. Too, being fascinated by natural history, Jefferson wanted to learn as much as possible about the geography, flora, fauna, and native peoples. To explore the route, he engaged Meriwether Lewis and George Rogers Clark, able men from his own county of Albemarle, Virginia, whom he knew and trusted. Imagine the daily risks. Often, while the rest of the party poled or paddled, Lewis wandered on foot observing flora and fauna, collecting specimens of new species. More than once the party was attacked by a grizzly. They suffered frequent illness. Upon reaching the snowcaps of the Great Divide, they discovered that passage by water would be impossible. Although discouraged—in fact Lewis may have experienced emotional devastation—they pushed on to the Pacific and, in all, made untold contributions to current knowledge.

Although not fraught with such physical dangers, real learning is a journey of exploration, daring, risk. It takes daring to explore a literary text such as William Faulkner's *The Sound and the Fury*, the first section of which is told confusedly by a thirty-three-year old idiot. It takes daring to consider rationally the advantages and disadvantages of democratic socialism, especially if you've been raised by parents and teachers who abhor or merely tolerate socialism in any form. Besides involving the acquisition of knowledge, higher education is the consideration of possibilities, no matter how far afield they may seem at first. Otherwise, how would we sustain our hope for a better world? How would we hypothesize a cure for AIDS?

Most college writing begins with exploration: reading, observing, note making. In history you might study Thomas Jefferson's writings, consider apparent contradiction between his keeping of slaves and his declarations about individual liberty, and write an essay presenting your conclusions. In biology you might observe the behavior of turkey buzzards hovering about a road-killed deer, make entries in your field notebook, and write a formal report of your findings.

In such work you develop your own conclusions from your own observations; that is, you detect patterns and compose meaningful interpretations. After detailed note making of your observations and thoughts, you select the essential information and ideas, examine them from different perspectives, think up as many credible interpretations as you can, select the most promising, and focus and arrange the material for your essay or report. The more curious and daring you become in this process, the more you discover and enjoy.

EXPLORING

WRITER
Develop strategies for
    reading, thinking, writing
Gather information and ideas
Make notes
Explore by writing

CONCERNS
Strategies for Exploring
Topic
Intention (Focus)
Voice (Persona)
Audience
Information
Ideas

Paying Attention

How is it that some students make fascinating observations even about such everyday happenings as turkey buzzards eating a road-killed deer? The observers sit undetected and watch intently, observing the carrion banquet, the patterns of behavior, the pecking order, the vultures' reactions as a dog trots toward them from a nearby farmhouse. They notice how buzzards are similar to and different from ourselves as social beings. They make notes. While it may be true that some people are just smarter than others, very often in a college class the difference between A or B work and C or D work is mostly a matter of figuring out what to do in a given situation or assignment—and doing it wholeheartedly. Being a good student means paying close attention—selective, focused attention—to the things around you, to information and ideas, to people and behavior, to language. In other words, to explore means to open yourself to possibilities of meaning in virtually any experience.

It means opening yourself to new methods of inquiry and collection. Some students naturally organize their notes and compose an essay or report systematically—

in a straight line, so to speak. Others naturally try out possible lines of thought by freewriting or some other method until—by intuition—they find a promising focus and direction. Some writing developed methodically may feel overly methodical or even lifeless to the reader, just as some writing developed intuitively may feel quirky and unfinished. What are your current methods? Might there be methods that will produce better results? Brainstorming, clustering, and freewriting are three of many intuitive methods that writers find useful. On the other hand, systematic outlining may be just the thing at certain junctures in your process for proceeding more systematically.

Brainstorming

An intuitive method of exploring engages the mind in thinking—as well as the hand in writing—as many thoughts as possible about a subject without pausing to consider their value or relationship or meaning. Continual movement without looking back can lubricate the mind, open it to the unexpected, and reveal both stored knowledge and new insights. Brainstorming involves the simple matter of listing rapidly whatever comes to mind about a subject. An individual or a group can use it. Executives in a manufacturing company might use it to solve a management problem. The boss might say, "Okay, let's brainstorm for sixty minutes to describe how the lack of childcare in our plant is affecting production and the well-being of our people. We've heard lots of comments lately. Something's happening. Is the lack of childcare our real problem? Or is it something else? John, you write everything down. And remember, we want to call out everything that comes to mind, no matter how dumb, and there'll be no criticism or discussion until after the brainstorming session. Kim, please keep time. After sixty minutes, we can decide if we need more time before starting our discussion. It may take longer for us to get in the ballpark with this. Okay, let's go."

Kim: "One of my best people has a three-year-old. She just can't afford full-time day care or preschool. Her aunt who lives nearby takes care of the kid during the day right now, but the mother doesn't trust the situation because her uncle drinks. The environment's not right for a kid, so the mother feels anxious at work. She's reliable but unhappy."

John: "One of my people has missed several days in the last month because her sister, who takes care of her kids, has been sick off and on. She's a good worker, one of my best, and it slows up the line when she's gone."

Esther: "I've got one that leaves her station every hour or so to call home, says this summer she has to leave her six-year-old with her twelve-year-old. That's scary for everybody, especially in that neighborhood. She glances up at the clock every few minutes. I can't blame her, but she's not doing very well. She's kind of slow on the job anyway, but she'd be okay if her mind was clear."

Maurice: "I've got a guy with four kids, all under ten. His wife died, and he's got no family here. They go to a church day care, but it's crowded and understaffed. The kids are restless at home, and the oldest is starting to have problems in school.

He runs over to the church at lunch to check on them, but you can tell he's over-whelmed. I mean people have to take care of their own problems, but this guy could be a supervisor if he didn't have so much on him."

Kim: "I've also got one who uses his childcare problems as an excuse to call his girlfriend—at least that's what the super told me the other day. He leaves his station three or four times a day. He does have childcare problems because his girlfriend works, too, but it's complicated and getting worse."

Boss: "I don't think the problem is childcare at all. I think it's the way people spend their money these days on all kinds of stuff they don't need. Like that woman in Maurice's division that always complains she can't afford day care and then shows up last week driving a new car—well, not new, but I mean new for her. People have got to get their priorities straight. We're paying top dollar—I mean as much as we can without going broke. What do these people want?"

Maurice: "A lot of my people make only three dollars or so above minimum wage. That's hard to live on these days. Everything's so high. They—I mean we—do have a good benefits package, though, for sure, one of the best."

Boss: "We're in business to make money. A childcare center here would cost us an arm and a leg. People need to take care of their own personal problems. If they don't, let them work somewhere else." [The boss can't keep from arguing his case.]

Kim: "My production's down 7% this month—and it seems to stem from a whole lot of little things. I have several mothers and one father with childcare worries who seem preoccupied with their kids. I've got the guy who calls his girlfriend. And I've got several people who've called in sick in the last month—more than I can remember in the past. People seem pretty stressed at work. One guy blew up at the super the other day, and I'd never heard him raise his voice before. We had a talk about it, and the guy said he was having problems at home. His wife needs to get a job so they can make ends meet, and they're both worried about the two kids, five and three. I think there are other problems, too, but that's just my intuition talking."

Boss: "How are things in shipping, Sam?"

Sam: "Like clockwork. No problems. One of my drivers asked me the other day if his kid could ride with him this summer. She's seven. I said, sure, I don't see why not. He said his wife works at a fast food and there's no way she can bring the kid with her."

Boss: "Geeeez, Sam. That'll never work. And what about liability? Our insurance doesn't cover riders. You know that. Imagine if the papers get hold of it. They'll make mincemeat out of us."

Kim: "Remember, Boss, we're brainstorming."

Boss: "Okay, sorry. I broke my own rule, didn't I."

So far, these executives are just scratching the surface of their company's problem, but they're making progress revealing their observations and, of course, their various points of view. John lists furiously, trying to capture the essence of each comment, as they attempt to define and understand the apparent problem before moving to solve it. Such a problem is no doubt very complex, involving efficient production, profits, wages, other matters of employee satisfaction, changing values, and who knows what else. They'll probably need several hours of such brainstorming.

As an individual working on a short essay, you can probably brainstorm a potential topic quickly—in perhaps thirty or forty minutes. A typical assignment is to read an article or essay in an anthology of readings and compose a 500-word essay summarizing and responding to it. Consider the situation of a typical student, whom we'll call Francesca Jones. She read an article that proposes free day care for all single parents who make less than $30,000 a year. The author of the article proposes a plan for complete funding of such day care with tax dollars. The student writer was not so interested in the issue of economics as she was in the issue of how we as a culture raise our children. She was pretty mixed up about the issue, just as nearly anyone would be, and she had some strong feelings. So, she began by brainstorming, letting her thoughts spill out onto paper.

Francesca Jones's Brainstorming

- *One parent, preferably the mother, should devote herself full time to raising her children at least until the age of five.*
- *I hate economics.*
- *Big reality: Lots of single parents with no source of income except welfare or work.*
- *I despise welfare for anyone who can work because it makes people dependent and not self-sufficient. Their children grow up like that, too.*
- *Is that really true?*
- *How can a woman stay home with kids and not be on welfare?*
- *Duh. I don't know.*
- *Having a plan for day care assumes there's no other solution.*
- *So, how can moms raise their kids and not be on welfare?*
- *You said that. So? This is brainstorming. Shut up.*
- *If they're married and the dads work.*
- *What if the dads don't make enough?*
- *Do the women have to work then?*
- *People spend much more than they need. What if we lived on a lot less? What if we didn't have TV, cars, BBQ grills, and other stuff?*
- *Can we return to a simpler life? Was life really simpler back then? When? Olden times—I mean, maybe, the 19th century on farms and stuff.*
- *But it's too idealistic to expect us to return. We've got huge cities with people living in apartments.*
- *There's no solution to this. It's too hard.*
- *Maybe I don't have to solve the problem for everyone. It's too much.*
- *Maybe I can just solve it for me.*
- *I'm nineteen. I'm a part-time student. I work part time. I spend as much time with Jesse as I can, but Mom takes care of him at least six hours a day. She and I disagree about discipline. She smacks his butt*

sometimes, which I hate, but I hate to bring it up because what would I do without her? But really—I want so much to raise him myself. But if I don't get my education, then I won't be able to provide well for him and be a good role model, too.

◆ *That's it. I have to make clear to Mom just how I want him raised and make sure she agrees. But how can she change? She used to smack me, too. I mean she's raised four kids of her own. It isn't fair to her to be spending so much time with Jesse when she could be having her own life now. She doesn't spend hardly any time painting, and she loves to paint.*

◆ *I'll never get this paper written. Yes, you will. Keep going. I'm frustrated. You should be. Shut up I told you.*

◆ *Harrington said to look at our own values and try to understand where we're coming from on our topic. Okay. Okay. I know I think parents should raise their own children. So how can a single parent like me make a go of life and raise Jesse? The author of the article proposes a whole plan. Maybe I can come up with a personal plan of action. So, I need to look at college, income, personal life, and especially raising Jesse.*

◆ *Income. I don't have anything except being able to live with Mom and Dad and working part time. Maybe I could work nights while Jesse's asleep. But won't that make him anxious if he wakes up and I'm gone? He sleeps pretty well. Maybe I can talk Moses into letting me work from 8 to midnight six nights a week. That would be 24 hours a week—about $144 less taxes and all that other good stuff. Maybe about $110 a week, $440 a month. Not much these days. Shut up and keep going.*

◆ *Okay, so I'm working while Jesse's asleep. I can spend late afternoon and early evening with him every day and all day Sunday. I can take him to the park, read stories, feed him, take him shopping. Shopping. Can't be much shopping—especially as something to do. Simple life, remember. Try to live on less. So what if I guarantee myself from 4 to 7:30 with Jesse, when he goes to bed and I go to work.*

◆ *School. I can be with Jesse each morning from 6:30 to 8:30. Then I can go to classes and study from maybe 9 to 3. If each class takes about 12 hours a week, maybe I can squeeze in three classes. Or maybe I should take just two, so I don't get so overwhelmed and stressed. Kids feel stress, too. They seem to know whenever something's going on.*

◆ *But you can't write a college essay on a schedule of stuff like this. Who'd want to read it?*

◆ *Values. What values do I have that are driving my thinking process right now? I'm struggling to raise my child in the best way I can and get an education without compromising either.*

◆ *You have to compromise. You're already compromising by letting Mom take care of Jesse when you're at school and work. Yeah, but I'm realistically, practically working things out in the best possible way instead of just letting things go as they are. Isn't there an essay in here someplace? No. Shut up. Okay. But stop sniveling and keep going.*

◆ *Wait a minute. I remember when we read some of Thoreau's* Walden *in Mr. Jimenez's class in high school. In fact, I think I saw an excerpt in our reader for this class. Thoreau said, "I went to the woods because I wanted to live deliberately." That always sticks with me. We talked about what he meant, but there's probably a lot more to it. Yeah, here it is, that same passage. "I went to the woods because I wanted to live deliberately." That's sort of what I've been thinking about. Not going to the woods and living in a cabin—although that would be great—but making choices deliberately, on purpose, consciously I guess is what I mean, instead of going along with things as they are. So, maybe I can write on that, with Henry's quote as my theme.*

◆ *I can still bring in stuff about childcare and even mention the other article, but I'll focus on Thoreau and how what he says makes sense in my life right now.*

◆ *People who've grown up on welfare aren't making choices. I'm not blaming them or their parents. But it's like they don't have any choices or don't think they do—when maybe they do. Off the point, honey. You're not writing about welfare. You're writing about living deliberately. Yeah, but maybe it's not off the point. Maybe I can use it as an example to help make my point.*

◆ *I need to start writing. Let's see.*

Jones's Fastwriting

In Walden *Henry David Thoreau says, "I went to the woods because I wanted to live deliberately." What he means is he wanted to make choices in his life, to control the things he could control, and learn what really matters. He chose not to eat meat, for instance, just because everyone else in his town ate meat. He thought about it and decided to eat beans instead. (He said he ate a groundhog raw, but I think he meant that as a metaphor or whatever for experiencing things at the moment, for following his natural impulses, which is another issue.) I think the main problem with America today is we don't follow Thoreau's advice. Instead of living deliberately, we just go along with what everyone else does and suffer the consequences. Only we don't even know they're consequences. We just do what we do. Like raising kids, for instance. Even lots of married couples both work because they think they have to have all this stuff and they dump their kids at day care or leave them with a neighbor or whatever. If people are going to have kids, they need to plan how to raise them right. A lot of our problems in America, like in the schools for instance, happen because kids aren't raised right. Parents expect the teachers to be parents and discipline and nurture their kids better than the parents do themselves because they're not around*

much, always working or playing golf or working on the car. And cars. Peo-
ple think they have to have two expensive cars when they could get along
with one cheaper one or in cities not have one at all. And it's the kids who
suffer, not being raised right, and then the society pays for it later. Having
kids is a choice, not a given, and raising them right is a choice, too, which
not many people make, I'm sorry to say.

I can't change the world, but I can make some deliberate choices in
my own life, especially having to do with my son Jesse. I didn't actually
choose to get pregnant. It just happened. So there was a case of my going
along with things as they are instead of choosing to protect myself. But
when I found out I was pregnant, that was a different story. My parents were
furious and wanted me to have an abortion, but I wouldn't have it no matter
what. Something deep inside me made me know I couldn't kill that child. It
was my destiny sort of to give birth to him and raise him. Of course back
then I didn't know if it was a boy or girl. But it was also a choice. My
boyfriend was freaked about the whole thing and bailed. I mean he hasn't
even seen Jesse, though it would be fine if he did. I told my parents I was
having him and that was that. No adoption either. He was my child and I
would raise him. When they heard how serious I was, it took awhile, espe-
cially for my dad, but they sort of realized they had a choice, too. They
could continue to freak and disown me or whatever or they could support
me as my parents and help me get through it all. I'm very grateful because
they've helped in so many ways. Dad even came into the delivery room with
me and Mom, because I asked him to, and I was so happy I cried. I didn't
even feel embarrassed. It was weird and great at the same time. I'm lucky,
you know. My one sister is still bummed about it, but my other sister and my
brother are real supportive, too, though they all live kind of far away.

Speaking of choices, which is my point really, I want to make good
choices for me and Jesse. Things haven't been all that good recently. Mom
has to spend too much time with Jesse and I don't like the way she disci-
plines him sometimes. She smacks him on the butt sometimes, and I just
don't believe in that. I believe you can discipline a kid just fine with firm,
fair talk and punishments, but not physical punishments. Physical punish-
ments teach kids that violence is okay, and I don't believe it is. So, I want to
make two deliberate choices. I want to talk honestly with Mom and Dad
about discipline and I want to work out my schedule better so I can spend
lots more time with Jesse and still work and go to school. Like Thoreau
talks about, I need to think consciously about what matters and then con-
sciously do certain things and not others. Like I can plan but to live delib-
erately I have to follow through with it, too. That's really the deliberate
part. I have to live my plan. I also have to keep at it even if I fail sometimes
which I probably will.

Life is choices. Sure, there are lots of things we can't control. But
there are lots more things we can control than we usually do. I'm deter-
mined to make good choices for Jesse and me and to raise him right, with

lots of attention from the one who loves him the most, me. Sure, I'll have to give up some things, but it will be more than worth it for both of us. I made straight A's in high school. Maybe I'll have to settle for B's in college. But it will be worth it for both of us. Can I get anywhere in a career with B's? Maybe I need to talk with some of my teachers or a counselor. I do want a good four-year degree in nursing. Can I even do that part time?

Notice how Jones moved naturally from brainstorming to fastwriting. In brainstorming she opened her mind and spewed her diverse thoughts onto paper. Suddenly Thoreau popped up and she felt a connection with her interest in making sound choices, especially in raising Jesse. She allowed herself to entertain this thought and to fastwrite a draft based upon it. While not yet a solid working draft, her fastwrite shows signs of focus and coherence. In fact, with some thoughtful rewriting, she can transform it into a draft suitable for bringing to a group session at the drafting stage. Many writers find it takes less time and effort to brainstorm and fastwrite, as Jones did, than to try to write a piece "right" the first time through.

Freewriting and fastwriting

In writing parlance, freewriting is an intuitive method of exploring that involves writing freely without stopping, usually for a predetermined length of time. You write down everything that comes to mind. You don't reject anything. You don't go back and reread until after the time is up. You keep going. Your brain warms up, so to speak, and unexpected thoughts pop up. You can use freewriting at any point—to clear your head of a nagging problem, to reveal your interests, to uncover a focus, to explore pros and cons, whatever. Some writing teachers begin each class with five minutes of freewriting. Their students write whatever appears from their minds and hearts. In writing so freely, they express their immediate feelings and thoughts, and clear the mind's way for class work. It's like running a couple of laps before soccer practice. Some teachers would call Jones's fastwriting (above) a *focused freewrite*, because instead of writing whatever came to mind about virtually anything, she wrote freely on the specific idea she'd discovered while brainstorming. While some teachers call this writing *focused* freewriting, I call it fastwriting. It means writing freely, as Jones did, but with a focus or specific purpose already in mind. As you'll see in Chapters 7–9, your written responses to drafts are fastwrite*s*. You write them freely and quickly, as in freewriting, but you follow certain guidelines rather than writing whatever comes to mind no matter how far-ranging. Sometimes I freewrite, especially in my journal. Other times I fastwrite. They feel quite different, so I give them different names.

Clustering

Clustering or *mapping,* also an intuitive method, is a fascinating variation on brainstorming. It's called *clustering* because instead of writing a list, which is usually linear, you write your topic in the middle of a blank sheet of paper and create clusters of ideas and information around it. You draw a short line out from it and then brainstorm in a cluster whatever ideas and/or information come to mind. After you've created one cluster, you return to the center, draw another line outward, and brainstorm another cluster. It's not hard to fill a page in a few minutes. Because your ideas and information appear in clusters visually, it's sometimes easier than in regular brainstorming to see connections between things you might not have thought were connected. And of course critical thinking involves, among other elements, the seeing of relationships and patterns. Francesca Jones realized immediately that Thoreau's *Walden*, which she'd read parts of in high school, offered guidance in writing about her desire to make deliberate choices in her own life.

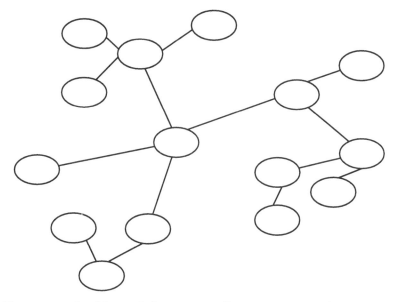

Try out new intuitive techniques—as well as more systematic ones—even if you've tried them before with little success. Your commitment to writing as a college student will almost surely generate new breakthroughs in your techniques, habits, and attitudes.

Freedom and Discipline

Peter Elbow teaches writing as a conscious interplay of freedom and discipline. Each of us can benefit from learning more about both. When starting a writing project, after you've done your reading and other research, allow yourself the freedom to discover and record thoughts as they occur. Keep writing quickly, without going back to rethink or revise. Engage parts of your brain that might otherwise be left out of the exploratory process. Open doors to possibility. Write down even the dumb ideas. If you get off the subject, keep going for awhile; your mind may be guiding you toward a new insight. If you're convinced something is true, explore wholeheartedly the possibility that it's false. Look at your material from different perspectives. Later is the time to evaluate, select, and arrange things. Later is the time for discipline.

Many students enter college with the mistaken notion that good writers and good students write a piece perfectly the first time, that they attend at once to everything. To help break students of such counterproductive perfectionism, some writing teachers require students to freewrite or fastwrite on a computer with the screen turned off. The exercise trains them to keep thinking and writing freely, without going back to rethink or revise. Such writing helps quiet the voices in our heads saying "not good enough." Allowing the time and means to explore openly will almost always produce better material.

Likewise, applying discipline, rereading notes, sorting through possibilities, deciding a promising focal idea, selecting and arranging illustrative and supportive material, outlining, however tentatively at this point, will help prepare you to launch a good working draft. In Jones's fastwriting above, she allowed herself the freedom to keep going. At the end, for instance, she tacked on the passage about sacrificing A grades. In her next draft she chose to develop that point for a whole paragraph. Notice, too, that while moving along freely, she also kept pretty well focused, as though her mind was naturally exercising a certain discipline to keep her on the subject. After letting her fastwrite settle for awhile, she read it over carefully, making notes about her main point and how she intended to develop it. She produced a plan or outline—one method of discipline—to guide her in (re)drafting.

Jones's Outline

Main Idea: Life is choices. Good choices are hard choices. To live well is to live deliberately. Thoreau: "I went to the woods because I wanted to live deliberately." I want to make good choices for my life and my son Jesse's life.

- ◆ *Having a kid is a choice*
  - ◆ *Birth control to protect yourself*
  - ◆ *Whether to have the baby*
- ◆ *Raising a kid well is a choice*
  - ◆ *Talk honestly with Mom and Dad*
  - ◆ *Schedule more time with Jesse*
- ◆ *Good choices require sacrifice*
  - ◆ *Grades*
  - ◆ *Extended college*
  - ◆ *Social life*
- ◆ *Sacrifice is worth it*
  - ◆ *Living my values*
  - ◆ *Raising a good person*
  - ◆ *Contributing to society*

Collaboration at the Exploring Stage

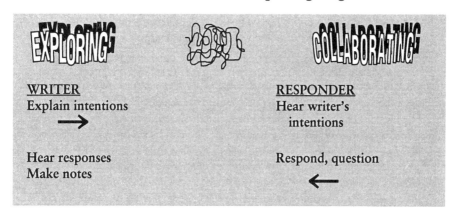

WRITER
Explain intentions
→

RESPONDER
Hear writer's
   intentions

Hear responses
Make notes

Respond, question
←

To help illustrate the process of collaborating in the exploring stage, I include work by the student Maj-Britt. (She requested I use her first name only, pronounced as if May-Britt.)

In her course each student chose a subject of special interest to investigate and write about for the entire first semester. Maj-Britt chose the role of the unconscious mind in our lives. Having had an unusual experience that had virtually transformed her, she wanted to understand it further and explain to others what had happened.

The first paper was supposed to be a vivid story of a person or experience that might have caused the student's interest in the subject chosen for the semester. Maj-Britt chose to write about her memorable encounter with John Red Elk, medicine chief of a Plains Indian nation. (She and I changed his name to protect his privacy.) She began by writing freely what came to mind. In reading it, you'll see starts and stops, as well as notes to herself about what she might do later—in drafting her piece.

Maj-Britt's Exploratory Writing about John Red Elk

I am not an Indian. All that was my reality turned upside down in 1989. In late January of that year I first met John Red Elk, Medicine Chief. I would never return to my old life.

As I sat in the humble sweat lodge, becoming one with the warm moist earth, I listened to the ancient sounds of his language. He reached out to me; made jokes and laughed amid the old sacred songs and chants. I sat before this man who loved his Creator with all his being. With tears streaming down my face & falling silently to my hands and lap, I became an eagle. My heart and my spirit soared.

Later that evening this mysterious man talked to us of his life, his people and his work. This gentle powerful man spoke only to me; our eyes & our spirits held us captive for hours. We both became aware of the interested crowd of listeners in the room. I felt a deep shyness as John made a joke and said he needed to rest.

Our relationship grew as we talked for hours. He out West and me 2000 miles away in Virginia. In the month of March John would return, but before his longed for arrival he shared many stories and parts of his life w/ me. Only later would I really know the many secrets he could never share w/ me, a white woman, without bringing me deeply into his world. So deep that I perhaps could never leave.

He talked of the spirit world; the dream time; the value and beauty of all life; the hardships and deep sorrows of his people; the many vision quests, long nights alone in the mountains, without food or water for four and often seven days singing the ancient songs and chants of his people communing with the Creator and other spirits of light and appeasing the spirits of darkness. He knew them both.

John spoke of visions of our future together. The elders of his tribe were against us being together. They would not allow John to marry me. John began talking of passing on his medicine; he would soon find the one who would become the new medicine man of his tribe; Perhaps his son, but there were problems—his son drank alcohol and that could be dangerous. John would go to Canada & pray for one week and then he said "I will know!" I knew he could never leave his chosen way and told him that his people needed him. I did not tell him that . . . . (?) This man whose gentle side was all I knew responded w/ great passion

"I am man first, I am chief, I am warrior, I have earned my power. I take what I want. No one tells me what to do!" (Well, that did it. I fell in love with this powerful man.) I could not have dreamed of a greater, more powerful romance.

The relationship continued to grow and by the time he arrived in late March, I knew this strange, passionate, proud, spiritual man more intimately than I would have imagined. You see, John loved my heart and my spirit. I had never known such a spiritual connection could exist between two people.

"The gifts I give you won't be material gifts," he said and I began seeing visions and being shown many things in my dreams.

I did not understand much of what happened to me, nor did I do any special meditations or chants. I simply prayed that I be shown the highest truth, the very purest truth. I couldn't settle for less now!

I was so at home following the native am way. It was soon time for John to return to his people and I was left with so much I could not begin to understand or explain. John had a life time of learning the way of the Indian. He was chosen by his people to become a medicine man when only a small child. With his medicine he knew how to handle energy and work w/ the spirits. I did not. There was much to learn.

I thank & honor this man and his people because through them I found my spirit, the light and the truth I sought, in the God of my people. The God of Abraham, Jacob and David.
    Aho.

NOTES: [NOTES TO HERSELF]

IMPORTANT—What about my summer out West, the Sun Dance, where this 50 yr old Indian was transformed to a young man of 20.
—His mother
—His elders
—His sons
—His other life—different now
I found I was not an Indian. This gentle and powerful way belonged to John not to me.
His world is not my world. It belongs to the Indian.

We may share, we may enter, we may taste, but if we stay, we risk much.
Bring John's world and presence to these people.
It is early morning [SHE'S STRUGGLING TO BEGIN]

As I sit high on a hill in the Blue Ridge Mts of VA I am aware of the gentleness and power of the earth beneath me—my body—my finger tips reach down toward the still wet grass of the early morning mountain meadow and my eyes travel to the blue cloud filled sky above and I remember . .

A day much like this (or the same as this) in 1989 when all I had ever known as reality was turned upside down (was questioned)

NOTES: [A NOTE TO HERSELF]

JOHN told me his spiritual name. This was his way of giving me the gift of his trust.

Rawness
transformed
I saw

State specifics [A NOTE TO HERSELF]

I was suddenly alone w/ him

Like many writers, Maj-Britt was stuck, not sure how to focus or where to begin a draft. Notice her attempt to create a setting in the present, sitting on the grass in a mountain meadow, thinking back on her experience. She'd wanted to bring her reader into the scene with her—but there were so many possibilities. The experience obviously meant a great deal to her, and she'd struggled to make sense of it.

Though stuck, she'd made progress toward starting an actual draft. Caring so much about her subject, she continued to feel a strong intention to write. She'd produced five handwritten pages, including some notes to herself about writing.

Exploring with Your Group

Don't underestimate the power of talking with your group—not so much to get ideas from them as to create possibilities in your own thinking by exploring aloud in the presence of willing listeners. As they question, respond, and support you, you're almost sure to discover new insights. The main purpose of each scheduled session with your group is to generate the desire, insight, and ability to produce better writing.

GROUP SESSION—EXPLORING STAGE

Leader	Convene the session. Invite the raising of unsettled issues. Orchestrate resolution. Review procedures for the session. Call for each member's special intention for the session.
Member	Declare a special intention for the session.

(15 sec. each)

Leader	Designate the first presenter. During the session, keep time. Ensure that each writer and responder follows guidelines.
Writer	Explain your main intention—focus, main ideas and information, intended audience.

(3 min.)

Responder	Listen.
	Make notes.
	After the writer finishes, explain your experience of the
	    writer's presentation: what the writer says, what seems
	    effective, what you want to know more about.
	Give a full, honest response. It's fine to repeat, as needed,
	    what other responders have said.

Writer	Listen.
	Make notes.
	Say almost nothing except "Thanks."
Leader	Allow time for the writer to complete notes.
	Repeat the process for each responder.
	Designate a timekeeper while you (leader) present
	or respond.

IF CONFLICT ARISES

Leader	Talk constructively with whoever appears aggressive
	in the conflict.
	Help restore civility.
Advocate	Talk constructively with whoever appears
	defensive in the conflict.
	Help restore civility.

Leader	Invite the raising of unsettled issues.
	Orchestrate resolution.
	If necessary, consult your instructor.
	Close the session.

Maj-Britt Talks with Her Group

Althea (Leader): "Okay, everybody, let's get started. How's every-body?"

Juan: "Well, I'm really worried about my mother. She's in the hospital for some tests, got intense pain in her abdomen. I was just there."

Maj-Britt: "What are you doing in class today, then? School must be pretty important. You haven't missed a day yet."

Juan: "Well, you know, I'm the first one in my family ever to go to college, and my mother and everybody always encourages me to do well. Even today, my mother said, 'Go on and go to class, son. I'll be fine. There's nothing you can do for awhile. They won't let you go with me for these tests anyway. I'll see you later this afternoon.' So here I am—a little ragged."

Mary: "I guess so. I thought I was having a bad day because my alternator gave out in my old Volvo. Hey, I'll shut up. Let's get started."

Althea: "Okay. Any unsettled issues about our group? No? Today we want to make sure everyone's on the right track for this first essay, which is a personal narrative that's connected somehow with our subjects of study for the term. Harrington said that above all we should produce vivid writing—tell a good story and tell it well. Let's declare our special intentions."

Mary: "I'm trying to understand this first assignment without getting too frustrated."

Juan: "I'm just trying to hang in here and pay attention."

Maj-Britt "I'm very frustrated with my writing, and I'm determined to leave here today with a focus. Whew. What a mess. I just can't get a handle on my essay."

Althea: "Well, let's start with you, Maj-Britt, and maybe the discussion will help you understand the assignment better, Mary. As you can see, I'm determined to serve as your noble leader."

Juan: "We could do a lot worse."

Althea: "Thanks. Maj-Britt?"

Maj-Britt: "Okay. Well, as you know, I'm writing about my special encounter with the medicine chief John Red Elk. Oh, yeah, my subject for the semester is the role of the unconscious mind in our lives, and I feel there's a big connection with John because he was so tuned into the different parts of himself. He lived everyday with things that were unseen. Forces and such that I can't begin to understand. In fact, he scared me sometimes with his awareness of things in me too, things I didn't know were there. There's so much to tell. What he looked like. Tall, handsome, mysterious. How he talked. How he acted. Strong and compelling but gentle, too, very kind and understanding. How he responded with anger and then resignation but kindness to me when the elders told him he couldn't marry me. How I felt about all of this. My own spiritual awakening as a result of being with him. My awareness that I wasn't an Indian. The tension between the two cultures as well as the sparks between John and me—or should I say fire? My heart still burns when I think about him, although I accept what happened. I mean it was a while ago. You know, a medicine chief is a big deal in a tribe with untold responsibilities to guide his people and help them maintain their wholeness. I guess what I got from the whole experience, besides a memorable experience with a remarkable man and his people, too, was a new awareness of who I am as an Anglo with my own spirituality. My spirituality is very deep, and somehow the experience renewed me. I'm stuck, though, on how to write it. Let me read some of my scribbling." [She reads from her brainstorming, freewriting, and other notes.] You can see it was pretty intense. What do you think I should focus on?"

Juan: "You're deep, Maj-Britt. I mean deep. Maybe you ought to go with me to the hospital this afternoon for some tests of your own."

Maj-Britt: "I will if I don't get some help with this paper, young man."

Juan: "Seriously, you had an amazing experience, an enviable one, like dating the Pope or something. Don't tell my mother I said that. Any-

way, you met this tall, handsome, mysterious man who fell in love with you and you with him—like in a movie. He seemed very spiritual. He seemed to have a big impact on you right away—like tears were streaming down your face. You both wanted to get married but the elders forbid him to marry you. He was angry at first, but you both seemed to know he couldn't leave his people. Could you have married him and joined the tribe? Would they have allowed that? I didn't understand that from what you said. Or didn't you want to stay there in Colorado or wherever it was? I'm fascinated by this man as you talk about him. But somehow the most important thing seems to be what you took away from the experience—what you learned or didn't learn or whatever. What you said about the God of Abraham. Not that you want to teach a lesson. The main thing is to tell the story well, as Althea said, tell a good story, but the focus could still be on his impact on you rather than on him so much. Good luck."

Maj-Britt: "Thanks, I need it."

Althea: "Good job, Juan. Mary?"

Mary: "Wow. It sounds like you had quite an experience. What a fascinating man. I know so little about Native American culture. Hearing you talk about it makes me want to learn about it. So, he's tall, handsome, somewhat dark skinned, and strong. Strong physically and mentally, I guess, though his strength seems shaken by his feelings for you. I can picture him clearly wearing jeans and a cowboy hat with a special band. Did I make that up? Was that right? Anyway, it's a shame they wouldn't let him marry you. Or is it? Could he have been happy, I mean really happy, away from his place in the tribe as, what was it, medicine chief? That's probably not relevant, but I was thinking about that. Even if he wasn't so special to his people, just a regular guy, it might be hard for people from two very different cultures to make it together. I guess that's not relevant. But anyway, I like how you tell about your feelings and his feelings. Like everything is all beautiful and sad and all mixed up. I don't know what else to say."

Maj-Britt: "Thanks. I think I could have been happy with him, but who's to say?"

Althea: "My turn, I guess. I get such a vivid picture of him—tall, dark, and handsome—sorry for the cliché—and very unusual. You're lucky, it seems to me, to have been able to have such an unusual experience—an experience of a lifetime. I mean, after such an encounter, after being so close to marriage with a special man like that, what else is there to live for? Just kidding. Anyway, while you were talking, I was thinking about what you must have been going through at the same time he was angry about the elders' decision. Both of you were all happy and sad and struggling with what to do. You might think about putting in even more about you. I don't know. What can a person say in 500 words?"

Maj-Britt: "Really."

Althea: "Maybe you should talk to Professor Harrington about it and see what he says."

Maj-Britt: "Maybe I should. I've been so frustrated trying to get something going. Thanks, you guys. It's great to be able to talk with you even though you're no help at all. No really, thanks."

Althea: "You're welcome. Who's next? Juan?"

[Each member takes a turn trying to explain his or her topic and focus for the paper, with responses from the others.]

Althea: "We're just about out of time. Harrington wanted me to remind us that our working drafts with copies for him and the group are due at the start of class Monday. Whew. There's lots to do. Any concerns about the group? No? Good. Mary, are you clear now about the assignment?"

Mary: "Yeah, thanks. I feel much better. I was actually doing the right thing but wasn't quite sure about it."

Althea: "I hope your mom is okay, Juan. Let us know, please."

Juan: "Okay, I will. Thanks."

Maj-Britt: "Thanks, everybody. See you Monday, with spectacular drafts."

Mary: "For sure. I think I'm gonna be sick."

Althea: "Get sick on your own time, girl. See you all Monday."

Really Stuck? Talk with Your Instructor

Maj-Britt's exploratory session with her group had helped, but she still felt stuck and decided to talk with me during my office hours right after class. When she appeared, I hadn't yet seen her exploratory writing.

Maj-Britt: "Professor Harrington, can we talk about my paper? I'm stuck. I had this wonderful experience that changed my life, and I've written several pages of stuff about it, but I just can't seem to get started on a draft."

Harrington: "What do you most want to get across to us as readers?"

Maj-Britt: "I want to show what an impact my whole experience with John Red Elk had on my life. I want to get at that, and I started with a scene where I'm thinking about it."

I read her exploratory writing (printed above). As she talked about her experience, I could see she wanted to focus on the man himself, but because she'd had so many memorable experiences with him, both out West and in Virginia, she didn't know where to begin selecting.

Harrington: "When you think back to your time with him, what scene appears most vividly?"

Maj-Britt: "Well, him speaking after the elders told him he couldn't marry me. And I guess his appearance and voice when I first met him."

> Harrington: "Put me in one or both of those scenes. Show me John Red Elk, so I experience him myself."
>
> Maj-Britt: "Okay. I'll see what happens. One of the concerns in my group was that maybe I should put more of myself into it than I had in my exploratory writings. What do you think?"
>
> Harrington: "Well, how's this for a squirrelly answer? I can't know until I see the actual focus of the draft you produce. It's your piece. Usually when I'm drafting, I make discoveries about what I really want to say and adjust the writing accordingly. You'll probably do the same. See what happens. Is that enough to go on?"
>
> Maj-Britt: "I hope so. Thanks. I'll give it my best."
>
> Harrington: "I'm sure you will. See you Monday. Call if you get really stuck."
>
> Maj-Britt: "Thanks for that, too. I appreciate the support. Writing can be a bear."
>
> Harrington: "Tell me about it."

In listening to her and looking over her exploratory writing, I could see she wanted and needed to begin with John Red Elk speaking. She had the makings of a draft; she just needed to voice her interest and intention briefly to discover her own direction. A brief conference, especially when you're stuck, can generate a powerful result. When you need it, seek professional coaching from your instructor.

A CONFERENCE WITH YOUR INSTRUCTOR—EXPLORING STAGE

Understand and honor your instructor's schedule and methods. Is it appropriate to meet during class, right after or before class, or during office hours?

Before meeting, reread your exploratory writing so you can discuss it. Think about why you might be stuck and what might enable you to move toward a draft.

If you must be late or cancel, contact your instructor beforehand if at all possible. If not, make contact as soon as you can.

If you're accustomed to a teacher's directing you, you may feel confused at first when your writing instructor asks you questions and looks to you for answers. It's your writing, and s/he'll probably work to draw out your thinking. Questions may address the adequacy of your exploration, your methods of inquiry, and your effectiveness in collaborating with your group.

When reading your exploratory writing, your instructor is looking for clues to your primary interests and insights. S/he's a highly-trained reader. Don't think s/he's taking your work lightly just because s/he reads quickly.

Understand that your instructor has many other students to work with, as well as committees, scholarship, other professional responsibilities, and personal life to manage.

Don't be offended if conference time is limited and focused primarily on your coursework.

Exploring on the Computer

Fastwriting, one of my favorite methods of thinking on paper, is especially effective on computer. The idea is to try out an idea or set of ideas by writing quickly. Without looking back to question what you've written, you invite your thoughts to spill out unhindered. Like many people, I type faster than I handwrite, so I have a better chance to capture my thoughts. Sometimes I find I can use whole passages of fastwriting in my draft. Even better, sometimes a piece of fastwriting becomes my draft. Because I've saved the computer files, I can retrieve the parts I need and download them into my composition. Also, I don't always know what passages I might need until I get to a certain point. It's nice to be able to search for and retrieve something at any time.

And of course writers use computers in much more sophisticated ways for locating information, making notes, and exploring thought. Your college library probably has its "card" catalog on computer. It probably stores back-issues of journals, magazines, newspapers, and perhaps other sources on CD-ROM. As part of their research, many students now explore the Internet and then print out or save to disk the sources that seem promising.

For note making as he studied promising sources, one of my students wrote a computer program that enabled him to type and file each note. Not only could he print out each note in the traditional format for notecards, but he could also sort scores of notes by category and print them out in bunches for contemplation or download them—quotations, paraphrases, and other recorded information—into his draft as he composed it.

If you feel lost or stuck, you might E-mail a group member or your instructor for guidance or for an appointment. When working at their computers, people tend to answer their E-mail promptly. I use mine daily for communicating with students, colleagues, and friends—on campus and beyond. Students at my college needn't have computers at home, although we encourage them to do so; they can sign up for an E-mail account in the computer lab, where they can send and receive E-mail messages whenever the lab is open.

Preparing to Draft

After you've written freely more pages than you'll actually use, then employ discipline to choose and arrange the passages that best advance the idea(s) you've discovered as your focus for the piece. You might outline these parts to create a plan for your first real draft. The main breakthrough for Maj-Britt was "Try starting here."

WRITER
Explore further as needed

Plan to explore and draft in plenty of time for scheduled response sessions with your group. For a typical 500-word college piece, the exploring and drafting processes may take several hours each—not including reading (or other preparation) and note making. The more you put into each process on your own, the more you'll gain from responses.

HIGHLIGHTS

EXPLORE ABUNDANTLY WITH DARING
AND PATIENCE

MAKE EXTENSIVE NOTES

KEEP IN MIND THE CURRENT STAGE

EXPERIMENT WITH METHODS FOR EXPLORING

CULTIVATE BOTH FREEDOM AND DISCIPLINE

DISCUSS YOUR INTENTIONS WITH YOUR GROUP

INVITE THEIR QUESTIONS, RESPONSES, COACHING

WHEN NEEDED, SEEK COACHING FROM
YOUR INSTRUCTOR

6

Drafting
Composing Your Working Draft

Drafting Freely, Expecting to Rewrite

Think about learning to serve in tennis. You have to allow your body to move naturally through a unified series of movements. If you think much about each movement by itself, you won't even hit the ball, much less develop a serve. If you prefer a musical analogy, think about playing a passage of music. Music is the rhythmic flow of notes in succession. If you think much about each note separately, you play notes but not music. As you begin drafting, write fairly quickly to keep the flow of mind going. Even if you're working from a plan or outline, allow yourself freedom to take a new direction. It may lead to a breakthrough in your grasp of the subject. Writing should be a process of continuing discovery.

While drafting, keep your mind focused on your main intention: expressing a particular message in order to transform a particular audience. At this early stage, don't distract yourself with concerns about grammar, usage, spelling, punctuation, and other mechanics, or even about refinements of style. Every time you stop to check spelling or to think of the exact word you need, you take your mind away from the drafting process. Trust that later, in redrafting and refining, you'll find the precise word, smooth out the flow of sentences, and correct the spelling. The mind deals effectively with only just so much at a time. Allow yourself the benefits of working in stages. Many professional writers, by assuming they'll rewrite exten-sively, compose the first draft rapidly. Many don't go back and reread but rather keep moving forward even if they realize they've moved away from their original line of thought. They allow the mind to follow a new direction, to uncover new pos-sibilities of insight or expression. Or they renew the original direction if it seems more promising. I recall one writer saying, "If I have only three hours in which to write something, rather than write it once for three hours, I write it three times for one hour." I also want to acknowledge that we're all different and that no one method of drafting works for all writers.

WRITER

Draft freely
Expect to rewrite
Redraft as needed

CONCERNS
Strategies for Drafting
Intention (Focus)
Voice (Persona)
Audience
Selection
Arrangement
Development

Drafting Is Hard

This stage of drafting and redrafting is the hardest stage for most writers. You struggle to produce writing that works as a whole. You struggle to focus on one purpose and a specific audience that together help you struggle to determine voice, arrangement, and development. Sometimes the more you write, the more possibilities you discover, and the harder it is to make choices. Even when you think you've achieved a draft in which all the parts contribute to the whole, it's hard to be sure. You're so close to it yourself. You haven't tested it on actual readers. And your college instructor's expectations are probably more rigorous than what you're accustomed to.

Your Intention—Your Focus

When reading your writing, professors generally expect evidence that you're thinking critically about your subject, gathering available information, considering different interpretations by experts, and drawing conclusions responsibly. In order to demonstrate such, you'll have to narrow the scope of your writing considerably more than you may be used to. Let's say for composition class that you're writing a 500-word essay on a social issue. Your professor has specified that you're to base your essay on your own experience and thought, but you're not merely to narrate an event. You're to develop an idea. You've decided to write about child abuse, partly because your mother verbally abused you. You suspect that other members of your group haven't experienced child abuse first hand, and there's a lot you want to tell them. But to compose a successful college essay, you'll have to choose one main point to reveal. One possibility is that although abused children may experience abusive behavior as a predictable occurrence, they feel little security. They develop insecurities that may undermine adult relationships. Many carry a lifelong fear of trusting others. Focusing on one main idea—here a long-term effect of child abuse—fosters critical thinking both in selecting the idea itself and in developing the idea substantially. The rigorous thinking expected of college students offers a new level of challenge, and that's the point.

Given this point, you might wonder why your instructor doesn't choose to read and respond to your drafts, instead of having you work in your group. S/he could readily say, "I don't see a focus yet" or "You're trying to cover so many points that you're not saying enough to convince me about any one point" or "It seems like you want to focus on why parents ought to listen more attentively to their children, but you haven't quite gotten there yet." Your instructor puts you on your own for the same reason the tennis coach doesn't stride out onto the court during a crucial match and serve for a player. Tennis is not about the coach playing but about the player playing. You develop grace under pressure only by being out there facing your opponent.

Thinking Is Hard

In some ways writing takes much more of you than the most vigorous tennis. It engages all of your faculties, especially language abilities—reading, listening, thinking, speaking. I remember years ago hearing E.D. Hirsch say, "You can only write so well as you can read your own writing." You as the writer must somehow comprehend how your writing comes across and what it means to readers. That's a complex reading ability that you can't possibly learn except by *doing* it, just as you can't learn to play tennis except by playing. Granted, your instructor, one on one, can help you learn how to read your own drafts and revise effectively. In doing so, however, s/he—who is a trained professional reader—might be conceptualizing your drafts for you, thinking for you, depriving you of the struggle necessary to learn to do it yourself.

The Wall

It's common in drafting, especially if you care about the subject, to come up against a blockage—something that stops you. Marathon runners call it the wall. Somewhere in the seventeenth or eighteenth mile they experience a sudden awareness that they can't possibly endure twenty-six miles. Trained runners know this will happen, know their bodies and minds are playing a trick, and simply keep pounding on.

When writers hit the wall, any number of things might be happening: fatigue, dwindling confidence in the value of the piece, inadequate ideas and information to work with, anxiety about unfinished math homework, awareness that dinner needs to be cooked, and many others. Unlike marathon runners, writers can take a break and sometimes should. Many seasoned writers have learned that even when a piece is generally going fine and will turn out fine, they nearly always hit a blockage at some point and must act in ways that work for them. When you come up against the wall, try various strategies and discover what works for you.

Years ago in graduate school when I'd come up against a blockage, I'd be so dead set on completion of a paper that I'd try to muscle my way through. I'd write and rewrite the same sentence over and over and over until—it just didn't work. Finally, I'd get so frustrated and fed up that I'd leave the room and just do something else to escape. While running or mowing the grass, something would happen. My mind would clear and I'd see new possibilities for advancing my essay. It took me a long time to realize I could create such breakthroughs by doing deliberately what I'd been stumbling upon unconsciously in the past. I learned to allow myself short breaks periodically and daily exercise.

One summer I took off from teaching so I could devote full time to completing the draft of my Ph.D. dissertation. I'd been researching it for several years and had amassed hundreds of notes on 5" x 8" cards. I'd been composing for months, but the writing needed lots of work. My plan was to write from eight to four, exercise for an hour, spend time with my family, and then write from eight to midnight. Every hour or so I'd stop in mid-sentence and play my fiddle for five or ten minutes without thinking about my writing. Those little breaks really helped keep my head clear. At four I'd review where I was in my writing and begin my three-mile run through the woods behind our old house. I'd let my mind relax and yet muse about the writing. During the run something helpful would nearly always happen. Not only would I feel refreshed, but also I'd often imagine how I could advance the writing from nine to midnight. While being with my family, cooking, eating, washing dishes, reading a bedtime story, I'd focus on being with them and try to forget my writing. A friend of mine in graduate school claimed the secret of renewing the mind while writing was to make bread every Saturday morning no matter what.

Investigate with your group and experiment with possible strategies for jumping the wall.

Redrafting Freely, Expecting to Rewrite

After completing your first draft, use a disciplined eye to evaluate how the parts work together to advance the main idea. You may have to draft again. That's the nature of writing. Try not to be discouraged. The result will be much better pieces of writing, better grades, and a greater ability to write successfully in the future. Make notes about your draft and create a plan for redrafting. As you redraft, again allow your thought to develop freely and naturally. Let the ideas and information take on a life and shape of their own. Your focus, your selection and arrangement of material, and your means of development should be more and more obvious to you and therefore more available for effective revision as you proceed. Let the writing carry you along. Train yourself to use the interplay of freedom and discipline by making an agreement with yourself. If you're a perfectionist who keeps rewriting the same sentence over and over, who just can't seem to move on through a draft, then grant yourself freedom to move forward imperfectly. You can come back later and refine the text. If you're a free spirit who can write endlessly but who hates to go back and revise, then grant yourself discipline to rework your draft. Somewhere between the extremes of freedom and discipline you can find a balance that works for you. Remember that your instructor wants to coach you in developing more effective habits and techniques. If you get stuck, phone, E-mail, or visit during office hours. Or get some coaching from a group member.

Completing Your Working Draft on Schedule

The course depends on your being prepared for each group session. If you're one who needs pressure to perform, make sure you feel that pressure well before your working draft is due to your group. I tell my students that the deadline for bringing the working draft to the group is the most important due date. If you compose a good working draft, which for some of us requires working up quite a sweat, the other stages of the process usually follow with relative ease.

Remember that a good working draft needn't be refined in style or proofed for grammar, usage, punctuation, and mechanics—those processes come later. But the writer has made considerable effort to focus on a main idea, to arrange the parts sensibly, and to develop each part credibly. The writer has also worked to create a tone of voice that fits the intended message and serves to transform the intended audience.

Drafting on the Computer

While drafting, I sometimes fall back into my old perfectionist pattern of trying to make each sentence the best that it can be before going on to the next. Such revising, which takes lots of time, slows my thinking to a crawl. The computer helps me walk forward because it offers the simple, invaluable gift of my being able to come back later and make changes where I want to without having to redo the whole piece. After composing a first draft, I make a printout and read it whole to see if it suits my purpose. If it pretty much does, then I go back into the computer and revise that same draft.

More often, my first draft just doesn't suit because it's too broad in focus and doesn't embody my intention. It's likely that I don't even understand my intention until after I've written at least one draft. So, I compose an entirely new draft, and then another, and then another—until I feel satisfied that I've discovered and embodied my intention. I save each file in the computer and on disk, and I save printouts of each draft, in case I need a passage in my final version. I rarely know what I'll need until I've completed the piece. And I save anything that might serve me in future pieces as well.

If you bog down completely in the muck of drafting and need a tow truck, you might E-mail a group member or your instructor for on-line discussion. You can attach your draft electronically to the E-mail note, so that the recipient can read what you've written and write back to you. Before doing so, decide thoughtfully whether you've spent enough hours struggling with the composition of your draft to justify seeking help. While your instructor wishes to provide aid when needed, s/he also wants each student to cultivate independence and self-reliance. Writing does require considerable time alone—with the brain in turmoil.

Making Copies in Time

Allow plenty of time for making printouts or photocopies for your group and, if requested, for your instructor. It's not fair or acceptable to hold up the group process by being late (except of course as a result of an uncontrollable turn of events such as a flat tire or ill child).

HIGHLIGHTS

DRAFT AND REDRAFT FREELY, EXPECTING
TO REWRITE

KEEP IN MIND THE STAGE YOU'RE WORKING IN—
SEE YOUR DRAFT WHOLE

TRY NEW METHODS

WORK FROM A PLAN BUT DON'T LET IT HOLD
YOU BACK

COPE WITH THE WALL

USE THE COMPUTER AS A DRAFTING TOOL

BE RESPONSIBLE FOR YOUR OWN LEARNING

MAKE COPIES IN TIME

IF YOU'RE REALLY STUCK, SEEK HELP

7

Drafting

Learning to Respond at the Drafting Stage

Considering Your Working Draft Realistically

Before presenting your working draft for responses from your group, read and reread it thoughtfully. Be guided by these questions: (1) What have I tried to accomplish? (2) How well have I accomplished it? (3) What must I do to improve it? Make yourself aware of its strengths and weaknesses. Prepare yourself intellectually and emotionally to reduce potential for defensiveness. Mark passages that make you feel even the least bit uncomfortable. In reading a draft of my own, I often experience little nagging feelings at a certain phrase or sentence or paragraph. Almost always, these are the passages where other readers (my wife, for instance, who never fails to point out a weakness in my prose) feel the need for revision. Because I've already allowed myself to feel those feelings, I'm more receptive to their responses.

Preparing Yourself for Helping Others

A draft is the writer's potential creation in the process of being realized. Notice the importance of *potential* and *process*. As writer or reader in the drafting stage, you want to employ your vision of possibilities. What potential is the piece attempting to realize? What point is it struggling to make? What feeling is it trying to evoke? Such questions demand your most generous attention. Through genuine attentiveness to one another's writing, your group can help each member discover techniques that engage and instruct readers.

Collaboration requires you—and each member of the group—to give your interest to another's work, whether it seems inherently interesting or not. I'm not talking about false praise, but rather attentiveness, no matter what the subject. Nearly any subject can be made interesting—if written about with a fresh perspective and if read with curiosity and a generous spirit. As a writer, you want to bring the best working draft you can muster. As a reader, you want to bring the best working attitude you can muster toward group members and their working drafts.

Inviting Inner Struggle

Working in a group helps you in the necessary struggle to conceptualize your own drafts and the drafts of others—to see and understand them as whole pieces of writing. You and the other members develop yourselves a great deal more than if you depended on the teacher to prescribe revisions for you. Each time you hear someone's draft read aloud or read it with your eyes, you struggle to conceptualize it as a whole. It may be incomplete, disorganized, or lacking focus, as many drafts are. You work to grasp what's there and imagine what the writer perhaps intended but failed to express. This process prepares you for conceptualizing and composing your own drafts.

Each time you struggle to articulate a meaningful response to another's draft, you develop your ability to think and express yourself constructively. You gather appropriate language, you order your thought, and you speak your mind. As you observe others struggling to do the same, you develop your ability to listen, read, make notes, and think, as well as to grasp and make sense of various perspectives. You develop understanding and empathy.

Each time you read your draft aloud, you discover new ways of hearing your own voice—and other elements—present in the writing and missing from it. As you receive responses from your group members, one by one, you again develop your ability to listen, read, make notes, and think, as well as to grasp and make sense of various perspectives. You develop your coachability, your ability to receive help from others. And you develop your judgment as you struggle later to decide how to apply the various responses—sometimes conflicting responses—in revision.

Now I hope you see why the teacher's role shifts dramatically from playing in center court to coaching from the sidelines. When you're working in a writing group, you're in action for a whole class period—DOING—writing, reading, listening, speaking, thinking—developing all of these fundamental abilities of language. Working together, you share the struggle, along with plenty of coaching from your instructor. Why settle for less?

<u>WRITER</u>
Read draft aloud
  before giving copies
→
Give copies of draft

→

<u>RESPONDER</u>
Hear writer's draft
  without copy
Write impressions
Get copy of writer's
  draft
Study writer's draft
Write response

The Key to Responding at the Drafting Stage

For responding to a draft at this stage, you learn to explain to the writer (1) your own relation to the piece and the extent to which you feel transformed into the intended audience, (2) the voice you perceive, (3) what the piece says whole as well as your experience of the piece whole, (4) what the piece says in each section as well as your experience of each section, (5) what strikes you as especially effective, (6) what you want to know more about, and (7) your parting thoughts.

HEURISTIC for RESPONDING

YOUR RELATION TO THE PIECE

YOUR TRANSFORMATION TO INTENDED AUDIENCE

VOICE (PERSONA) YOU PERCEIVE

WHAT THE PIECE SAYS WHOLE
YOUR EXPERIENCE OF THE PIECE WHOLE

WHAT THE PIECE SAYS IN EACH SECTION
YOUR EXPERIENCE OF EACH SECTION

WHAT STRIKES YOU AS ESPECIALLY EFFECTIVE

WHAT YOU WANT TO KNOW MORE ABOUT

PARTING THOUGHTS

This is not merely a checklist of things to cover in a response but rather a *HEURISTIC*. A *heuristic* is a guide for systematic exploration of an issue or solution of a problem. In classical Greek and Roman culture, orators used *heuristics* to prepare formal speeches. The *heuristic* enabled them to explore their thinking on the subject in all dimensions required and expected for persuasive oratory. More than just a set of steps or procedures, a *heuristic* is GENERATIVE. Applied properly, it generates rich thinking and feeling. It stimulates the mind, body, heart, and soul towards a worthy purpose.

Learning to apply this *heuristic* for responding at the drafting stage is the single, most important lesson in learning to work together on writing. At the end of my courses in composition, my students write a 500-word, final-exam essay to demonstrate their accomplishments as writers. They also write a 500-word response to a student's working draft (which I provide them) to demonstrate their ability to apply the *heuristic.* I expect the response to generate in the author of the working draft both the desire and the information needed to revise effectively. My request is that you memorize the elements of the *heuristic,* internalize them with frequent practice and review, and thus refine your ability to generate rich, useful responses that your group members look forward to and embrace.

Making Notes While Hearing or Reading a Draft

To help you learn to study and conceptualize a working draft, whether your own or someone else's, I include the first working draft of the essay by Maj-Britt, whose exploratory writing appears in the chapter "Exploring." An Anglo-Norwegian American, she had lived briefly on an Indian reservation in the West and experienced an intimate but doomed relationship with a medicine chief. While reading it for practice, make notes that empower you to attend to it, think about it, and recall its features.

When responding at the drafting stage, attend only to the big picture. I designate two different class sessions for this process, each with its own set of purposes and procedures (described later). In the first session, the writer reads the draft aloud, before giving copies to responders, so they can listen and write their strongest impressions without noticing surface errors such as spelling. Even when you as a responder do receive your copy, you'll need to overlook smaller matters of style and correctness, so that you can concentrate on voice, focus, arrangement, and development. While the writer reads aloud, write down especially

KEY IDEAS, WORDS, AND PHRASES YOU HEAR
IN THE DRAFT

With these notes you create and record your awareness of what
occurs in the draft.

OBSERVATIONS AND INTERPRETATIONS OF
THE DRAFT

With these notes you indicate what you notice in the draft and in
your own experience of it—how the writing affects you, including emotional impact, images evoked, any confusion created, and
passages you like.

Maj-Britt's Draft

In reading Maj-Britt's draft, imagine she's a member of your writing group
awaiting your response.

John Red Elk: Medicine Chief
by Maj-Britt

*"I am man first, I am chief, I am warrior, I have earned my power.
I take what I want. No man tells me what to do!" This was the passionate
response of John Red Elk when he recounted the decision of his elders
regarding our marriage.*

*Much more gently now, this strange, mysterious man began talking
of giving up his medicine, passing it on to another and living a quiet life
with me. There was sadness in his once powerful voice now for he could
never leave his destined way.*

*My heart and my spirit ached for him. I believe he sought refuge in
me. I had the feeling that he sometimes didn't have the strength to battle
with the spirits any longer or to be responsible for the needs of his people.*

*His passionate strength and gentle smile brought me back to the time
I first met John Red Elk. Someone introduced us, but we needed no introduction. He stood tall and straight in his large black cowboy hat, white
shirt, blue jeans and boots. The only part of his clothing that spoke of the
Indian was his beaded belt. His face dark & clear, his mouth straight yet
gentle, his nose large, straight & strong, his eyes shining & clear almost
black, his hair bluish black, pulled back & tied with leather at the nape of
his neck, he wore the leather around his neck which I knew held his medicine pouch. He became every inch the Indian Medicine Chief. "So, you're
Maj-Britt, I been waiting for you girl," he said. I could not speak. His eyes*

held me captive while his hand reached for me. His voice belonged to an Indian of long ago. I was in love!

I followed John into the sweat lodge that day, I followed in his native way; to the vision quest, the Sun Dance and more. I was at home in his world. He brought me into the spirit world & the dream time. John shared with me the beauty, hardship & sorrow of his people. We became one as he lay beside me singing his ancient songs and talking of secret vision. "Pull down the shades now; the darkness has come," he said. The evil spirits come out at night you see. John knew the spirits; the spirits of light and those of the darkness, too!

It was soon time for John to return to his people, and I was left with much I could not begin to understand or explain. John had a life time of learning the way of the Indian. He was chosen to become a M.M. by his people when just a young boy. With his medicine he knew how to handle energy and work with the spirits; I did not. There was much to learn!

I found I was not an Indian. This gentle powerful way belonged to John not to me. I could share, I could taste, even enter his world, but to have stayed I would have risked too much.

I will always honor this strange, mysterious man and his people for through them I found my spirit and the joy, truth and light I sought in the God of my people. The God of Abraham, Jacob and David.

Aho.

My Notes in Response to Maj-Britt's Draft

While I'm listening to a working draft read aloud, with or without my having a copy, or while I'm reading one silently, I underline or circle things, draw lines between things, and make extensive notes. Wanting to demonstrate the note making process for my students, I asked for a volunteer to read a draft aloud. Maj-Britt raised her hand. Below are the notes I took on the blackboard while she read. As you read my notes, you may wonder why I wrote down mostly (1) key ideas, words, and phrases present in the writing, and to a much smaller degree (2) my thoughts and feelings in response to the writing. In listening to or reading a draft and making notes, I prepare more effectively for my response if I do much more of (1) than (2). By thorough noting of (1) key ideas, words, and phrases that are present in the draft, I empower myself to recreate my experience of the writing afterward. During my speaking or writing to the writer, my notes on (1) enable me to recall and recreate (2) the responses I had while listening.

Maj-Britt

John Red Elk. Medicine Chief. His nation. "I'm a man 1st. I am chief. I am warrior. I take what I want. No man tells

me what to do."
Then much more gentle. Mysterious. Strange.
Sadness.
My heart ached as he talked of peaceful life.
CONTRAST
Passionate strength & gentle smile
1st. mtg.   FLASHBACK
Needed no intro
White shirt blue jeans boots hat.
beaded belt
black hair pulled back   dark & lean
nose large + straight
leather lacing—treasured medicine
pouch

"So, you're Maj-Britt. I've been waiting for
you, girl." —BLACK ELK SPEAKS
Sweat lodge—followed John
sun dance
"dream time"
"spirit world"
beauty, hardship, sorrow
became one "Pull down those shades now."
lay beside me
spirit visions
light + darkness

time to return to his people

he had a lifetime of learning
young boy
energy   HANDLE?
spirits

much to learn—I was not an Indian
CONTRAST HIM VS HER

share/taste/enter—BUT to stay
I risked too much
I honor him and his people.
God of my people.
Aho!

My Response to Maj-Britt's Draft

As a sample, here's the response I gave to Maj-Britt's draft after she finished reading it aloud. (In typing, I recreated it pretty nearly as I'd spoken it.)

MY RELATION TO THE PIECE
WHAT THE PIECE SAYS WHOLE
MY EXPERIENCE OF THE PIECE WHOLE
WHAT I WANT TO KNOW MORE ABOUT

Throughout the writing I can feel your intense fascination and involvement with John Red Elk and his culture, especially Native American spirituality. I don't know what it all means, but I feel how deeply meaningful the experience was and is to you. You seem to have entered the Native American world, so to speak, as an outsider, done your best to live within that world, and then realized you had to come away, had to return to your own world. It seems you returned transformed somehow. You seem to have learned much that informs your life now. I feel that—and I'd like to know more about it.

MY TRANSFORMATION TO INTENDED AUDIENCE

I envision your readers as people like myself who know something about Native American culture—but not much really—who become curious to know more about Indian spirituality and the role of leaders such as John Red Elk. We also become curious to know about the experience of an outsider such as yourself, particularly since you developed such a close relationship with a medicine chief. It's like falling in love with the president. I become sympathetic to his plight and yours.

VOICE I PERCEIVE

Your tone is generous, appreciative, caring. The voice compels me to listen, to contemplate, to think about my own spirituality. There is longing in it too, the longing for something lost as well as for something else not quite found. There is also confidence and hope—belief that the speaker's own spirituality is rich with possibilities not yet fully explored.

WHAT THE PIECE SAYS IN EACH SECTION
MY EXPERIENCE OF EACH SECTION

As the piece begins, I hear John Red Elk making a declaration of his authority: "I am a man first. I am chief. I am a warrior. I take what I want. No man tells me what to do." My first impression is of his strength and per-

*haps arrogance. Then you describe him as gentle, mysterious, strange,
compelling. The whole piece is a study of contrasts: contrasts within his
character, contrasts between his world and yours, contrasts in time.*

*After the opening, which apparently takes place just before your
decision to leave, you flash back to your first meeting with him. He seems to
have known you were coming, because he says, "So, you're Maj-Britt. I've
been waiting for you, girl." That reminds me of a scene in the book* Black
Elk Speaks, *maybe from the introduction, translated into English from the
words of the nineteenth-century Oglala Sioux medicine chief Black Elk.
Apparently Black Elk had no worldly knowledge of the arrival of a particular visitor and yet "knew" he was coming. I don't remember the details.
John Red Elk seems very compelling, very inviting as a man, as a personal-
ity, as a tribal leader—so inviting that you felt you were "in love." You followed him into the sweat lodge, the sun dance, the "dream time," and the
"spirit world." The two of you became as one in spirit. He seemed
acquainted with things of the spiritual realm, things of light and darkness. I
was uncomfortable with the word "handle" to describe his abilities; it
seemed to trivialize his gifts as a spiritual leader, which I'm sure you don't
intend. The other language throughout seems very respectful.*

*After a time together, he seems to have wanted to marry you and set-
tle down to a quiet life, but he needed to return to his people—apparently
to fulfill his responsibilities as medicine chief—I guess a person doesn't
just walk away from that job, that calling. It seems the elders rejected his
request to leave. His words at the opening of your piece sound like a strong
declaration of his power or authority to do whatever he chooses, but he
doesn't seem to believe it fully—or he would have left with you. He accepts
his duty to his people.*

*In the end you realize you aren't an Indian. You honor him and his
people. You were able to "share, taste, enter" their world, but to stay
would have been to risk too much. I can't tell for certain whether you chose
to leave him or he chose to leave you or what. I certainly sense mutual
understanding of the issues for each of you.*

*You seem to have come away spiritually energized, excited to reunite
with the God of Abraham, so to speak—to follow your own native spirituality.*

WHAT STRIKES ME AS ESPECIALLY EFFECTIVE

*At the start I get a vivid picture of John Red Elk as a tribal leader
speaking in his own voice to the elders of the tribe. Later I get a vivid picture of his physical appearance when you describe his white shirt, blue
jeans, cowboy hat, beaded belt, long bluish-black hair, and distinctive
nose. I visualize, too, his medicine pouch hanging from a thong around
his neck.*

I like your use of sweat lodge, sun dance, dream time, and spirit visions—though I can only imagine what some of them refer to.

Dialogue puts me right there. For instance, "Pull down those shades now" and "I've been waiting for you, girl." It seems as though John Red Elk is speaking in his own voice.

In the end I'm struck by the "joy, truth, and light" available to you now in the God of your own people, the God of Abraham, Jacob, and David. Though you and he must part ways, you bring back with you energy that you didn't have access to before. How do I know that? I feel it in the writing.

WHAT I WANT TO KNOW MORE ABOUT

I want to know more specifics about your experience with John Red Elk and his people. I want to understand what exactly transformed you. Certainly you seem to have been transformed—and not just because you fell in love with an intriguing man.

I appreciate the mystery of Native American spirituality as suggested by your piece. I also want to know more about such phenomena as the "dream time" and "spirit visions," not that you can explain everything in the same piece.

I'm intrigued by your experience, and I look forward to reading your next draft.

Reflections on My Response to Maj-Britt's Draft

As a reader, I read to learn something and to feel moved—intellectually or spiritually or emotionally. In college you write mostly essays, reports, and other forms of nonfiction prose. Academic readers expect writers to focus specifically, to probe a subject deeply and thoughtfully, and to develop each point substantially and credibly. Maj-Britt had a unique and fascinating experience with John Red Elk, and I enjoy and appreciate her draft. At the same time, I feel a need for more definite focus and development, in part because near the end she brings up but doesn't reveal much about her own transformation. Two interrelated topics emerge in my mind: (1) her experience with John Red Elk and (2) her transformation as a result of her experience. I want her to understand my needs as a reader and at least consider them as she contemplates revision. I want to tell her these things in a manner that will encourage and guide her in rethinking her intention. I try to reveal appreciatively the content of her draft as I experience it. As a reader—not merely as a writing teacher—I feel the need for more about her spiritual transformation or at least about the cultural contrast between herself as an Anglo-Norwegian-American and John

Red Elk as an American Indian. In saying that to her, I want her to feel my genuine curiosity and enthusiasm about her transformation. I want her to see what I'm seeing in a way that is GENERATIVE. I want what I say to generate in her a further vision of what's possible in her essay—without my giving her direct advice. She's the writer, and she needs to struggle with her own thoughts and feelings about her subject. I don't want to declare what she should do, but rather to share my response constructively in a manner that helps open her eyes to what's actually there and what could be there.

Observing, Describing, Interpreting, Evaluating

As I mentioned earlier, Joe Strzepek taught me the value of distinguishing four main types of response to a piece of writing. We can (1) observe it performed (read it, listen to it read, see it as a play, etc.); we can (2) describe it without interpretation or judgment; we can (3) interpret it without judgment; and we can (4) evaluate it. Normally in our lives, these four activities of mind and heart occur at once in constant interplay. All too often in our experience with writing teachers, however, we are accustomed mainly to being judged. Some of my students report that their former teachers didn't seem to describe and interpret their work as much as mark it up and grade it. So what's the problem? Isn't that the writing teacher's job to mark and grade papers? Yes and no. There is value in learning what we've done wrong, but much traditional marking and grading have focused more on what's wrong than on what's working or what might work in a piece of writing. The things marked are often surface features of usage and mechanics, which do of course need attention. But the preoccupation in schools primarily with surface correctness such as spelling gives the false impression that good writing is primarily a matter of surface features.

Because teachers have tended to mark and grade papers based upon what's wrong, beginning college students often want to do the same when they begin working in writing groups. To respond effectively in the drafting stage, they must train themselves to suspend their need to judge what's wrong and focus on what is actually going on in the piece and in their own minds and hearts when they read. Joe Strzepek's four categories can be very useful in this training. They're also very useful, by the way, in learning to read literature such as poetry or the short story, by helping us focus on certain elements that we might otherwise overlook. The more research I've done on the matter of constructive responses to writing, the more I've come to see the power of description and interpretation in helping writers look toward effective revision. Notice that description involves the reader's observations of the form and content of the writer's text. Interpretation involves the reader's observations of his or her own thoughts and feelings while reading the writer's text.

DESCRIPTION:
THE READER'S "OBJECTIVE" SENSE OF THE
CONTENT AND FORM OF THE WRITER'S TEXT

INTERPRETATION:
WHAT TRANSPIRES "SUBJECTIVELY" IN THE READER
WHILE READING THE TEXT

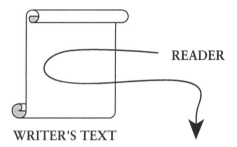

READER

WRITER'S TEXT

DESCRIBES AND INTERPRETS
WRITER'S TEXT

Reader-Based and Criterion-Based Responding

For your responses to produce optimal results, your group follows principles and guidelines that are like fundamentals in playing music. You practice them over and over until you internalize them and can perform them naturally. One basic principle is the distinction of performing, describing, interpreting, and evaluating. Another is Peter Elbow's distinction between reader-based responding and criterion-based responding. A reader-based response grows from the reader's actual experience of the writing, whether or not it fits preconceptions of what that type of writing is "supposed" to be like. A criterion-based response springs from preconceived expectations of what that type of writing is "supposed" to be like. A good response reports how the writer's text actually affects the reader in the act of reading. So it's primarily reader-based, but it may well include preconceived criteria.

READER-BASED RESPONSE:
REPORTS THE READER'S "NATURAL"
EXPERIENCE OF THE WRITER'S TEXT
(MOSTLY DESCRIPTIVE AND INTERPRETIVE)

CRITERION-BASED RESPONSE:
APPLIES PRECONCEIVED STANDARDS OR "RULES"
(TENDS TO BE EVALUATIVE)

In schools and colleges, criteria are often pre-established "rules" that are applied as judgments. They tend to create misconceptions about how readers actually do respond to writing, and because criteria are often presented as judgments, they tend to block thinking and understanding rather than open readers and writers to possibilities. We teachers are especially prone not to read student writing as an experience but to measure it against a rigid set of criteria. Students who are used to their teachers responding merely with a set of judgments tend to do the same when responding to the writing of their peers. I've observed that such responses don't teach student writers enough about how actual readers respond. It's not that I don't expect every teacher and myself, as well as every student, to develop sound criteria for effective academic writing. In fact, notice above how, in my reflections on my response to Maj-Britt's draft, I reveal criteria I expect in academic writing (even though her piece isn't "academic"). But students best develop such criteria experientially—mainly from involvement with writing and the responses of a variety of thoughtful readers who respond honestly and openly—rather than from mainly adopting and applying a set list of criteria.

An example of criterion-based responding that can undermine the actual reading process is the widespread expectation among teachers that shorter student essays contain five paragraphs: an introductory paragraph with a thesis that asserts three causes, or three effects, or some other trio of points; three body paragraphs, each developing one of the trio; and a concluding paragraph. Used skillfully, this formulaic structure can serve well for much academic writing, but it's not the only structure for an effective short essay. A teacher of English or history who expects the five-paragraph structure and essentially nothing else may respond less than enthusiastically to an exceptional piece of writing simply because it doesn't fit the preconceived structure. In other words, for that reader the criteria have become absolute and have virtually closed down the possibility of reading with sensitivity to other forms of good writing that well may accomplish the assigned purpose.

Perhaps you've noticed that in this book I use contractions to help create a conversational tone. My sixth-grade teacher Mrs. Randall and most of my other teachers along the way would be embarrassed. "Never use contractions," they declared. "Never use I." "Never begin a sentence with *and*." (I prefer the advice of my mother, who was also an English teacher: "Never use *always* or *never*.") You may feel as they do about contractions and be quite put off by my gross informality. I invite you to respond according to how you've been taught, how you've thought about such matters yourself, and how you actually experience uses of language and thought that may fall outside your usual expectations. (Stylistic choices such as whether or not to use contractions actually shouldn't come up until a later stage than drafting—the stage devoted to refining style—but I wanted to use a clear example to make my point here in the section on drafting.)

Do use your preconceptions about writing, your preconceived criteria, but don't allow them to block you from sensitive, thoughtful reading of your classmates' essays. If you're in my writing group and you're put off by my contractions, I want you to tell me—honestly and helpfully—so that I can decide whether or not to keep them. Frankly, I advise my students to avoid contractions when writing for teachers, prospective employers, and other people who might be put off by such informalities—to help prevent distractions from the actual purpose of the writing. You can probably tell from my writing that I don't wear a coat and tie when I teach. But when I address the board of directors of the college, I do dress up. Why? Because they expect it of themselves and others who attend their meetings. If I didn't dress up, some of them would notice my clothes as inappropriate and perhaps think about my inappropriate dress rather than my message to them about a faculty concern.

So it's not so much what you say in a response to writing as how you say it and where it comes from within you. If you say to me, "I've always been taught not to use contractions in formal writing, and your using them distracts me from what you're saying," you're being honest, direct, and useful. You're letting me know exactly how you as a reader experience my contractions. Said that way, it seems easier to swallow and more useful than if you said, "Never use contractions in formal writing." Let's say you're responding to a working draft of an essay that doesn't reveal its thesis—its main intention—until the final paragraph. It may be that throughout the reading, you can intuit the developing point and you don't feel at all confused. You feel enticed—pleasantly teased—toward understanding. In responding, you might say exactly that: "I like how your essay teases me along toward understanding and then reveals its full intention in the last paragraph." On the other hand, it may be that you do feel confused because the main intention isn't revealed clearly enough until the end. Then it's appropriate and necessary to say, "I felt confused through much of the essay because I wasn't sure what you were getting at until the very end. The confusion bothered me—distracted me from what is obviously a very important issue." Note how different this manner of responding is from, say, "You should always state your thesis in the opening paragraph, and you don't make yours clear until the end."

Responding as a reader reading—rather than as a teacher or reader judging—is much like the recommended method of communicating in any close relationship, responding from the point of view of *I* and *my experience*. In a personal relationship it's usually much more honest and palatable to say, "I feel threatened when you talk like that" than to say "You threaten people." The former is a statement of the one person's actual experience of feeling threatened. The latter is a judgment about the other person, declared as an objective truth. In response to the former, the other person is more likely to understand and empathize, whereas in response to the latter, the other person is more likely to feel and act defensive and not become sensitive to the message or the messenger. It's not just a matter of how the message is delivered, although method of delivery and tone are very important. It's partly a matter of the content of the message. In a close relationship one person may feel threatened by a certain tone or certain words of the other person, while someone else hearing the same tone or words might not feel threatened. In other words, it may not be true objectively, that the other person talks in a threatening manner. It's dishonest and certainly counterproductive, then, to make such a claim, just as it is when a teacher pretends—whether consciously or unconsciously—that there is but one way to structure a college essay.

Learn to respond as a thoughtful, sensitive reader in a manner that generates revision. The reader-based response offers the writer a "video" of the reader's experience—what Peter Elbow called "movies of your mind." In reality those videos are bound to be a combination of reader-based and criterion-based responses. It would be thoughtless and counterproductive to pretend that we don't have sets of criteria, say, for academic writing that are useful and necessary to know and apply. To develop yourself as a responder, become aware of your own preoccupations when reading others' writing and develop ways to express honestly as well as generatively how your preoccupations affect your responses. For instance, let's say the history essay you're reading contains illustrations drawn from the student writer's own experience. The personal material does seem effective—perhaps it touches you personally—and yet you also believe that such material is inappropriate in an academic essay. You might say something like "I like the personal illustrations. They get the point across vividly and move me emotionally. But I'm not sure they belong in an academic essay." That's a good reader response because it's generative as well as honest. It gives substantial information and leaves the decision up to the writer.

As Reader, Who Are You?

So, I invite you to take and practice the role of reader responding rather than judge. But what exactly is that role? If the piece is ultimately intended for a teacher, should you be yourself, so to speak, or should you project yourself into the teacher's role? I remember overhearing a student in a responding session say, "I don't know the word *fetus*. If I'm going to understand, I need for you to use a word I do know." The group called me over for a consultation. I was pretty sure everyone else in the group knew and used the word *fetus,* which is of course very commonly used in our society. First, I acknowledged the honesty of the response. Then I explained the writer's need to consider whether a word needs to be changed or defined in the text. Is it a technical term that needs a special definition as part of the writing? Is it a rare term beyond the immediate grasp of most intended readers? Or, is it a fairly common word but one that some readers may have to look up in the dictionary. *Fetus* is of course a commonly used word, one that this particular student needs to look up and learn. In this case the writer shouldn't oversimplify the piece, particularly given that, ultimately, the intended audience for many college essays tends to be educated adults or highly educated professors with expectations based upon their disciplines.

I include the *fetus* example because it helps us get at a tough challenge for many first-year college writers and readers. The audience for college writing is often a reader who is more educated and hence a more capable reader and writer than the student. This is backwards from the usual relation of writer and reader. Normally in our day-to-day lives, the writer knows more than the reader about the subject, and the reader reads in order to learn what the writer knows. In college, however, often the main purpose of writing is for students to stretch themselves both as readers and writers—to learn material in, say, psychology and to demonstrate that learning as well as critical thinking about the material. The members in your writing group serve as intermediaries who help you stretch yourself and learn to reach the higher levels of reading and writing expected by your professors, employers, publishers, and the like.

In order to help you stretch yourself, your group members must also stretch themselves as writers and readers. As readers and responders, they must combine their own grasp of academic writing with their personal thoughts and feelings. If they strictly try to imagine how a given professor or other audience might respond, they lose touch with their own responses. If they rely strictly on their own personal responses, as in the *fetus* example, they won't help you stretch yourself as you must for success in college. Frankly, it's a hard balance to achieve, especially in a class or group with a variety of students, some better prepared than others for the college experience. But my request is that you proceed with faith that the group process will work better than any other method. It can, and given commitment by all, it will. In my nearly thirty years of college teaching, I've tried many approaches, and nothing compares to working together.

Some college students, especially some who are well prepared for college, tend to write what they mistakenly think professors expect—highfalutin prose that almost no one likes to read because it's pompous, stuffy, unnecessarily pumped up with big words intended to impress rather than communicate. (Ken Macrorie called such writing *Engfish*.) A group member who is less well prepared can help such a student write more simply and directly—which is not to say less intelligently. Likewise, in the reverse, that user of big words can help other group members build their vocabulary as well as think more critically about each topic. Perhaps oddly, it's the variety in a group that often produces the most significant results—if all members are committed to their work, to the process, and to one another.

Validation and/or Revision

Responses to a working draft as a whole—with attention to the "big picture"—engage the writer as s/he struggles for focus (main intention), audience, arrangement, development, and voice. Through such responses, readers demonstrate how they experience the writing. They validate parts or all of the text as it is and/or evoke new possibilities for revision. The writer comes away with a keener awareness of what works and what doesn't. In your group, you as the writer experience three responses in addition to your own. It's a struggle sometimes to sort the information, to see where the responses coincide and where they deviate, and then to decide for yourself what and how to revise. In doing so, you learn how readers do respond, and you prepare yourself to anticipate how specific audiences—your history teacher, your employer, the readers of the area newspaper, and so forth—will respond to what you write in the future.

Such Responding Takes Practice

It takes training and practice to develop effectiveness in responding generatively. The tendency is firmly embedded in most of us to apply criterion-based generalities and *judge* the writing without actually *responding* to it. Your instructor will have special ways to coach you in following the guidelines for working together. While there are several key elements to be covered in each response, it's important that the response be connected discourse—one unified communication—rather than a few sentences addressing each element in isolation. Responding is an act of *creation*. I teach my students to begin with the first item—one's connection with the writer's text—to establish productive interaction with the writer from the outset. After that, the order of elements doesn't seem to matter as long as each element gets adequate coverage. The response should feel spontaneous, developing as a natural outgrowth of the reading experience. The challenge is very like learning public speaking. At first, the process may seem tense and unnatural, but in time things take their rightful place.

Maj-Britt's Revision

To revise means to "see again." With responses from her group and me, Maj-Britt rewrote her working draft several times. Much of what appears in the later draft (below) comes from the first working draft (above). Yet the two drafts are different. What differences do you notice that apparently sprang from "seeing again"?

John Red Elk: Medicine Chief

"I am man first. I am chief. I am warrior. I have earned my power. I take what I want. No man tells me what to do!" This was the passionate response of John Red Elk as he recounted the decision of his elders regarding his marriage to me. "No," they had said. "We forbid it." And then—much more gently—this strange mysterious man began talking of giving up his medicine, passing it on to another and living a quiet life with me. Sadness overshadowed his once powerful voice for he knew he could never leave his destined way. My heart and my spirit ached for him as he continued to talk of this peaceful and quiet life—this refuge—apart from his medicine

His passionate strength and gentle smile brought me back to the time I first met John Red Elk. Someone introduced us, but we needed no introduction. He stood tall and straight in his oversized black cowboy hat, white shirt, blue jeans, and boots. The only part of his clothing that revealed the Indian was his brightly beaded belt. His hair was shiny black, pulled back, and tied with leather at the nape of his neck. His face was dark and lean with prominent cheek bones jutting out beneath his almost black, brown eyes. His nose was large and straight except for the slight crook left by a once broken bone. His mouth was drawn in a straight line across his face. His chin was strong and proud. He became every inch the Indian Medicine

Chief as my eyes found the leather lacing around his neck, which I knew held the treasured medicine pouch. "So, you're Maj-Britt. I been waiting for you, girl," he said. "I been waiting a long time." His voice belonged to an Indian of long ago. I could not speak—I tried—I could not. His eyes held me captive as his hands reached for me. Still, words would not form in my mouth. My heart, my mind, my entire being was filled with this man; he occupied every cell of my body.

I followed John to the sweat lodge that day. And in the days and months to come I followed in his native way: to the vision quest, the Sun Dance, and beyond. I was at home in his world. He brought me into the dream time and into the spirit world. He shared the beauty, hardship, and sorrow of his people with me. We became one as he lay beside me singing his ancient songs and talking of secret visions. "Pull down those shades now. The darkness has come. The spirits are out there now," he said. John knew the spirits, the spirits of light and those of darkness too.

It was time for John to return to his people, and I was left with much I could not begin to understand or explain. John had a lifetime of learning the way of the Indian. I had not. He had been chosen to become a medicine man when just a boy. With his medicine he knew how to work with energy and with the spirits. I did not. I had much to learn. I learned I was not an Indian. I cried. I mourned the loss. This powerful way belonged to John, not to me. I could share, I could taste, I could even enter his world, but to have stayed would have risked too much.

I will always honor this gentle, powerful, mysterious man and his people for through them I found my spirit, and the joy, truth, and light I sought in the God of my people.

Aho.

My Observations about Maj-Britt's Revised Working Draft

Although her revisions perhaps seem minor, they created a major change in my experience of her piece. I applaud her for considering my responses and the responses of her group, and for keeping them in perspective. We'd observed that two themes emerged in her earlier draft: her experience with John Red Elk and her transformation that resulted from her experience. I'd mentioned the probable need to focus on one or the other. What she did was to add and change a few lines in the conclusion to intensify our understanding of her personal and spiritual response to her experience. I feel more deeply her torment at his decision to remain with his people at the expense of their relationship, and at the same time her gratitude for her personal and spiritual centering within her own culture. Besides this effective change in the conclusion, she brought clarity and unity in the opening by paragraphing thoughtfully and adding explanation. Also, in the middle of the piece she added more details to her description of John Red Elk, partly as a result of conversation with her group. So, she retained the integrity of her original working draft and at the same time unified and strengthened the piece.

HIGHLIGHTS

LEARN TO GIVE HONEST, HELPFUL RESPONSES:

(DESCRIPTIVE AND INTERPRETIVE)
(READER-BASED AS WELL AS CRITERION-BASED)

YOUR RELATION TO THE PIECE
YOUR TRANSFORMATION TO INTENDED
AUDIENCE

VOICE (PERSONA) YOU PERCEIVE

WHAT THE PIECE SAYS WHOLE
YOUR EXPERIENCE OF THE PIECE WHOLE

WHAT THE PIECE SAYS IN EACH SECTION
YOUR EXPERIENCE OF EACH SECTION

WHAT STRIKES YOU AS ESPECIALLY EFFECTIVE

WHAT YOU WANT TO KNOW MORE ABOUT

PARTING THOUGHTS

8

Drafting
Sample Student Responses

Cheryl Lewis' Working Draft

In the second semester of a two-semester course in composition, one assignment for my students is to select a short story we've read and write a 1,500-word essay about it, incorporating literary criticism, or other works by the same writer, or a concept from another discipline such as philosophy or psychology. The primary goal is sound critical thinking. Cheryl Lewis chose "The Story of an Hour" by Kate Chopin, a startling, unsettling little masterpiece of ironic fiction only two pages long. In it, the main character, Louise, learns that her husband has been killed in an accident. Her first reaction is shock and grief. But then she begins to feel a certain liberating if frightening lightness of being, the inexplicable lifting of some inexplicable burden. Her life swells with exhilaration, hope, independence, freedom. A short while later, when he appears at the door, she falls to the floor dead. People exclaim that she died of "the joy that kills." We as readers know otherwise. Lewis, having read and heard that Chopin's famous novel *The Awakening* deals with similar women's issues, decided to read it as well and produced the following draft.

[Dare to Be Free
Exploring The Awakening and "Story of an Hour" by Kate Chopin]
[Note: The original working draft was untitled]
by Cheryl Lewis

In the short story "The Story of an Hour" and in the novel "The Awakening," Kate Chopin explores the daring theme of personal freedom for women. In the 1890's, a woman's life was anything but free.

93

In "The Story of an hour" Louise was genuinely distressed when she heard of her husband's death. However, when she was alone, she felt a thought coming to her, one she knew was daring and unusual. When that thought finally came, it was the realization that she was free. "Free! Body and Soul free!" (pg. 72). This was a new and intoxicating thought for her. She never before dared to think of a life of her own, making her own choices, and having her own thoughts. I believe that she never would have dared this thought except for her husband's death. His death inspired her to look into her own soul. In that soul, Louise found a reason to joyfully live. It is very hard for us today to realize how daring and rare was the thought of freedom.

In the "Awakening", Edna is awakened to herself and to a world of self-exploration and personal freedom. She learns to swim and she becomes more emotional, she feels the experiences of life deeply. Ironically, the better she knows herself, the more she realizes that she is only a possession of her husband and she truly has no choices. Her husband treats her like an object, also. He doesn't spend much time with her, expects her to obey his every whim, and discourages her to think for herself. He is not emotionally involved with her at all and sees no need to be! She is compared to the beautiful objects he likes to collect. That is what she is to him, a beautiful object and he is baffled by her rebellious actions.

At this time in New Orleans, where "The Awakening" is set, women were legally the property of their husbands. Everything a wife had was her husband's when she married, including any money she earned and the clothes she wore. She was required, by law, to live with her husband and follow him wherever he decided to reside. She could not, without her husband's consent, sign a legal contract, appear in court, hold a public office, or make a donation. In other words, she had no right to her own life; it was her husband's decision where she lived, how she lived, and the friends she had.

In "The Awakening", Edna is tortured by the knowledge that she can never have what she wants, her freedom and her only love, Robert, so she commits suicide. I feel that Edna and Louise have much in common. Both are exhilarated by the idea of being their own person. Louise has glorious daydreams about the days that would be her own. Edna pretends that her life is her own. But when both women are faced with the sordid facts of their existence, both women choose death over living in captivity. Louise's heart gives out at the sight of her husband. I feel she chose to die rather than live in submission. "There would be no powerful will bending her in that blind persistence with which men and women believe they have a right to impose a private will upon a fellow creature." (pg. 72). How could she face living like that after her intoxicating taste of freedom?

Edna found a way to keep Leonce and her children from possessing her; she swam to her death in order to have her freedom. "She thought of Leonce and her children. They were a part of her life. But they need not *think they could possess her body and soul." She did not kill herself because she could not have her lover Robert, but because she had no choices in life, no freedom. In fact, her last thoughts were not of Robert, but of her carefree childhood.*

One hopes that, in our time of enlightenment, personal freedom is available to all men and women. Plus, we have many choices for women to escape an oppressive relationship. In Louise and Edna's time, freedom was an illusion and death was the only choice for them.

Linda Johnson's Response to Lewis' Draft

Cheryl: opening paragraph is good. The tone is good—the words explores and daring catch your attention. The last sentence is good, setting up for the saga.

Paragraph 2—I like how you describe Louise's thought of recognition of freedom here. The tone changes here to an excitement level or realization. I think you may need to describe Louise more—give background about her life w/ her husband. You may want to use the type of death he experienced and tie it in w/ some symbolism. (If there is any?) I would give an example with your last sentence to drive the point home.

Paragraph 3—First I have never read The "Awakening," but just from this small background here it sounds like a great story. Good use of words still. You continually repeat some of the same words to help the reader key back on the theme. Again here, I feel you need a small amount of background on Edna. I would like to see an example of her being more emotional after she learns to swim. Is there a parallel here? You know me, I like things like that. I would expand on some of the experiences of her life—the use of the word possession is very strong here. Grabs your attention. May want to repeat the word possession—to set it in hard in the mind. The husband sounds somewhat like some men today in the twentieth century. I would like to see a couple of examples here. Love the word choices in the ending sentences—whim, discourage, baffled & rebellious—gives you an idea that the husband really isn't in tune with his wife.

Paragraph 4—The tone changes here to give a reflection of hurt I think. It really shows how women were treated and how men thought of them. I would like to know the year here that we are talking about. I think you should expand and give some of how you know they were legally property. Really shows a sad state for women then. I would have not been able to put up with that type of life.

Paragraph 5—Continuing on a sad & realistic tone here. Good use of word torture. Who is Robert? Why is he her only love? May want to expand this concept.

Sad, that people chose death to be free, but it is a real concept—happens so many times today in this century. Louise dying—may want to com-

pare it to how the thoughts of "freedom" are and then that freedom being taken away.

Paragraph 6—Interesting concept of bringing the children in. Why does Edna feel her children possess her? Tone continues to be sad—but powerful because of the use of suicide to get freedom. May want to throw in some statistics on suicide in women linked to depression, etc.

Closing paragraph—good use of words—tone changes to hope. Expand on the choices for women today escaping oppressive relationships—I think that is needed to show the offset of suicide as the only option. May want to use a definition of suicide somewhere for effect & how serves.

Overall enjoyed your paper. It brings out an important point about the human heart and brain. It is very important for people to understand how humans make decisions such as suicide to escape whatever they feel they need to.

I would use some background in the beginning. I got somewhat confused about Edna, possibly because I have never read the story. Expand on some ideas and give examples in some places. Overall—very good—good theme choice. Gets your attention.

Joyce Broderick's Response to Lewis' Draft

Your writing in this essay is very good Cheryl. It has tone and good purpose. You explained in detail why the lady was happy after receiving word that her husband was dead.

In the second paragraph the lady held her composure until she was alone. When she was alone in her room she realized she was a free woman. This is when she became very excited over the thought of being free. She would now have full control of her life and not have to answer to anyone.

The third paragraph, you talk about a lady who is controlled by her husband. He treats her as if she is his prize possession. The lady in this story has no choices in her life. The husband makes all the choices and decisions; she is only one of his many beautiful collections. To herself, she is nonexistent.

I am so glad time has changed for women. I could not imagine living with a man that controlled everything in my life. I am woman! I'm surprised they didn't need to ask permission to be excused.

The fifth paragraph is very sad. You tell us how the lady committed suicide because she couldn't be with the man she really loved. In the days of Edna, a woman divorcing her husband was unheard of. The word divorce was not spoken.

Men controlling women is still not so uncommon. In the nineties a person would think things are different but in actuality it's a lot of people who still control each other. Men and women.

I'm not sure if Louise chose death or if it was the shock of seeing her husband alive that brought on the heart attack. I feel if she had had the choice she would have chosen to live. Being controlled would be better than death to most people.

Edna, I feel, was pushed over the edge by her husband and children. She felt like an animal trapped in a cage. The thing most people don't realize is there is always a way out of a bad situation. All it takes is a little positive thinking in place of the negative thinking. Think of all our options other than suicide.

I cannot believe death was the only option Louise and Edna had. Even in their day, it had to be another way out other than suicide. I don't think they weighed all their options out completely. I just cannot except that was the only way.

Michael Farruggio's Response to Lewis' Draft

Response to (untitled) by Cheryl Lewis. An essay on two stories by Kate Chopin on the lack of freedom of women in the late 19th century. In "The Awakening" and "The Story of an Hour," two women struggle with a lack of personal freedom. Freedom to make their own decisions, freedom to pursue a career. Freedom for just about any civil liberty. Women back then were almost slaves to their husbands.

The idea of making this comparison, of these two women's deaths, one dropping dead and the other committing suicide, is a great idea. Your point that both sort of chose death themselves is interesting. Louise's heart giving out, her being shocked to death by the sight of her thought dead husband after dreams of her new freedom and the acceptance of his death, seems like a bit of irony to me. I don't see this as her making a choice, I see this as a shocking eye opening ending, showing the reader the depth of her "acceptance" of his being gone forever. After all, it was the very end of the story, sort of a "wow" ending, the "joy that kills."

The paper is excellent. The way you laid out the paragraphs—the way it followed, flowed. I added margin notes to point out small critiques— these are just my personal points—dismiss them if you disagree. They are not meant to be brash, forgive me if they seem so. [Note: Here I include Farruggio's marginal notes, written on his copy of the draft itself.] *Paragraph 2: Identify Louise as the main character. What was this thought that came to her? How did it form? Paragraph 3: Identify Edna as the main character. What was her awakening? How did it form? Paragraph 4: Who is Robert? Is she having an affair? Introducing the quote might help set it. Paragraph 5: Who is Leonce? Her husband?* Summary comment written on the copy of the draft: *A very well thought out paper. Great idea for a comparison. It's a shame men treated women that way. I wonder if I would*

*have been a product of my environment and acted as badly, or would I still
be the "me" I know and be different? I also wonder how many men were
that way? Was it just the aristocracy? I believe I wouldn't have been that
way! Mike* [Note: Now we return to his main written response.]

*What of a title for this work? The joy that kills? The freedom of
death? ehh?*

*Paragraph 2—Louise? Maybe say who she is. It made me think
about it. Then lines 3 & 4 talk of her thought. I'd think it well if it were
described what this thought was, how it developed in her mind. This would
give your reader more insight into why she acted and thought the way she
did. After all—your reader might not have read this story.*

*Paragraph 3: Edna—again, maybe say who she is. I never have read
this book so I didn't know. Also—what do you mean by "awakened to herself?" Is she asleep, or dreaming, or did she have a self-realization? Can
you explain that as well as what did she think? Same as above I guess.*

*Paragraphs 4 & 5—Should these be connected? They seem to be on
the same book. At least the first sentence. And who is Robert? Is he an
affair, an old lover, a dead one? Then maybe go into a separate paragraph
with #6. That seems to compare the reasons for, and their deaths. That one
seems to stand out by itself in the second half of paragraph 5. Who is
Leonce in 6? I assume its Edna's husband.*

*An excellent well thought out essay. I really enjoyed it. I can't imag-
ine being like those men—even with my own personal thoughts on femi-
nism! Mike.*

Lewis' Next Revision of Her Draft

Dare to Be Free
Exploring <u>The Awakening</u> and "Story of an Hour" by Kate Chopin

by Cheryl Lewis

In the short story "The Story of an Hour" and in the novel, The
Awakening, Kate Chopin explores the daring theme of personal freedom
for women. In the 1890's, a woman's life was anything but free.

In "The Story of an hour" the main character, Louise, was genuinely distressed when she heard of her husband's death. However, when she
was alone, she felt a thought coming to her, one that was daring and
unusual. "But she felt it, creeping out of the sky, reaching toward her
through the sounds, the scents, the color that filled the air" (pg 71) When
that thought finally came, it was the realization that she was free. "Free!
Body and Soul free!" (pg 72). This was a new and intoxicating thought.
Always before, like all the good wives of that time, she had submitted to

her husband's will. She never before dared to think of a life of her own, making her own choices, and having her own thoughts. "She breathed a quick prayer that life might be long. It was only yesterday she had thought with a shudder that life might be long" (pg 72). She never would have dared this thought except for her husband's death. His death inspired her to look into her own soul. In that soul, Louise found a reason to joyfully live. It is very hard, today, for us to realize how daring and rare was that thought of freedom.

The Awakening *is the story of Edna who was raised to behave and obey at all times. She married at a young age to a man twelve years older. She endures her life of obeying others until the summer she and her husband, Leonce, vacation on Grand Island, Louisiana. She finds herself spending time with Robert, the son of the resort owner, and a Creole woman, Adele Ratignolle. For the first time in her life someone is listening and encouraging her to have her own thoughts. Edna breaks out of her shell, discovers self worth, and seeks her place in life. She learns to swim and begins to experience life profoundly. She focuses these new ideas and emotions on Robert and becomes infatuated with him. Robert realizes they are falling in love and leaves in order to escape the dishonorable folly of a relationship with a married woman.*

Edna realizes that she is only a possession of her husband and children; she truly has no choices. Her husband treats her like an object. ". . . looking at his wife as one looks at a valuable piece of property . . ." (pg 4). She is compared to the beautiful objects he likes to collect. That is what she is to him, a beautiful object and he is baffled by her rebellious behavior. He doesn't spend much time with her; he constantly leaves her alone. "It's a pity Mr. Pontellier doesn't stay home more in the evenings" (pg 69). Edna is expected to obey his every whim and is discouraged to think for herself. He is not emotionally involved with her at all and sees no need to be!

According to Margaret Culley, Professor of Women's Studies at the University of Massachusetts, during the time when The Awakening *was written, women were legally the property of their husbands. Everything a wife had became her husband's when she married, including any money she earned and the clothes she wore. She was required, by law, to live with her husband and follow him wherever he decided to reside. She could not, without her husband's consent, sign a legal contract, appear in court, hold a public office, or make a donation. In other words, she had no right to her own life; it was her husband's decision where she lived, how she lived, and the friends she had.*

In The Awakening, *Edna is tortured by the knowledge that she can never have what she wants, her freedom and her only love, Robert, so she commits suicide. "Despondency had come upon her there in the wakeful night, and never lifted. There was no human being whom she wanted near her except Robert; and she even realized that the day would come when he, too, and the thought of him would melt out of her existence, leaving her alone. The children appeared before her like antagonists who had overcome her; who had overpowered her and sought to drag her into the soul's slavery for the rest of her days. But she knew a way to elude them" (pg 113). She sees no possible escape from her predicament except death.*

Edna and Louise have much in common. Both are exhilarated by the idea of being their own person. Louise has glorious daydreams about the days that would be her own. "Her fancy was running riot along those days ahead of her. Spring and summer days, and all sorts of days that would be her own" (pg 72). Edna pretends that her life is her own. "Without even waiting for an answer from her husband regarding his opinion or wishes in the matter, Edna hastens her preparations for quitting her home on Esplanade Street and moving into the little house around the block (pg 83). "Whatever was her own in the house, everything which she had acquired aside from her husband's bounty, she caused to be transferred to the other house, supplying simple and meager deficiencies from her own resources (pg 84)

When Louise and Edna are faced with the sordid facts of their existence, both women choose death over living in captivity. At the end of "Story of an Hour," Louise's husband opens the door; he is alive after all. At the sight of her husband, Louise's heart gives out. I believe she chose to die rather than live in submission. "There would be no powerful will bending her in that blind persistence with which men and women believe they have a right to impose a private will upon a fellow creature." (pg. 72). How could she face living like that after her intoxicating taste of freedom?

Edna found a way to keep Leonce and her children from possessing her; she swam to her death in order to have her freedom. "She thought of Leonce and her children. They were a part of her life. But they need not think they could possess her body and soul." She did not kill herself because she could not have her lover Robert, but because she had no choices in life, no freedom. In fact, her last thoughts were not of Robert, but of her carefree childhood.

In our time of enlightenment, personal freedom is available to all men and women. Plus, there are methods for women to escape an oppressive relationship. There are private and government organizations to help people in need. There are shelters for battered women and some laws to protect them. The laws are more equal now to both men and women than they were in 1890. Women have all the basic rights; they can vote, hold office, make contracts, and lead their own lives. Women can earn a living and raise children alone. Alimony and child support can be obtained. It is not always easy, but there are options. In Louise and Edna's time, Freedom was an illusion and Death was the only choice for them.

Works Cited

Chopin, Kate. *"The Story of an Hour."* Literature: Reading, Reacting, Writing. *Ed. Laurie G. Kirszner and Stephen G. Mandell. 2nd ed. Fort Worth: Harcourt Brace, 1996. 70-72.*

Chopin, Kate. The Awakening. *New York: Norton, 1976.*

[Note: Lewis hadn't yet added Margaret Culley's work here. Also, she hadn't yet made her in-text citations conform to MLA style: (71) not (pg. 71).]

Reflections on the Three Responses to Lewis' Draft and Revision

As I reread the responses by Johnson, Broderick, and Farruggio, I'm struck especially by their honesty and thoughtfulness. Clearly they respect Lewis and seek to help her produce a better essay by taking time to report their many observations. While any one response may not seem "perfect" or "ideal" in applying all elements of the heuristic, each displays a willingness to do so, a willingness to engage fully in the challenging process of responding GENERATIVELY. And their impact on Lewis' essay is quite remarkable. Clearly, she took their responses seriously. She added several well-selected quotations from the story and the novel to illustrate and support her points. She cited Margaret Culley's work on the plight of women in the 1890s. She clarified, enlarged, and rearranged several passages, producing paragraphs that are better developed and balanced. I'm intrigued how her revision process displays much more than merely the addressing of points made by each responder. Throughout, Lewis has kept in mind, clarified, and intensified her original theme and spirit—as a result of the dynamic and in some ways magical interaction of the readers responding and the writer listening, pondering, and rewriting. Both processes—of responding and of rewriting—require months, even years, of attention and practice. Do your best and take heart.

Three More Sample Responses

Below are three more sample responses at the drafting stage. They display mainly description and interpretation, revealing to the writer primarily what the reader perceives and conceives. For simplicity, I include only the response and not the writer's draft. As in studying the above responses and their probable purpose and effect, keep in mind the *heuristic.*

Max Katz's Response to a Draft on Anorexia

mmmm . . .

Your paper really struck a chord with me—I know exactly what you're saying about ridiculous standards of beauty. It's almost a relief to see it in print—it's hard to argue with the pressures of the media that you're talking about.

So—your purpose is to inform & warn anyone of the dangers of media messages. Your tone is clear and sensible.

You start out stating the problem—unrealistic media images & the dangers they pose to young people. I wasn't sure exactly what your thesis was on the first time I read through the paragraph though. I like the "born losers" quote.

Then you go on to the actors/actresses & demonstrate the impossibility for even these people to live up to the desired image.

The next paragraph combines a) the changed beauty image and b) measurements. I don't really know what to do with the numbers you give but I suspect I am unusually ignorant of such matters. The last sentence of this paragraph brings up eating disorders, which merges into the next paragraph—which has a really strong quote about the absurdly young anorexic girl and info on eating disorder type things. The TV shows are a good reference & connection to daily life, even if I'm not sure how substantiated/well-grounded that comment is.

In the conclusion you go beyond the statistics and connect the issue to people in the world—it gives a nice sense of what can be done about the problem.

I was quite convinced at this point of the reality of the problem. I'd like to know which of the ideas in the paper were yours—you documented everything well but I couldn't figure out where the source info stopped & your thoughts started. Also, I want to know more about male young people & their media reactions to your topic—but I'd like to know to what extent older (say, middle-aged) age groups are affected.

Anyway—it all really rings true, and you've got some great quotes in there, too. Despite your calm tone, it's a stirring paper—the issue (I find, at last) is quite frustratingly ridiculous & I think you're doing a really good job with it.

Randall Nordstrom's Response to a Draft on the Difference Between Schooling and Education

I like the way you use the quote at the beginning to define what education is. Then you go on and define schooling and how it is different from education. You have clearly introduced your viewpoint by doing this. I like the point you make about how succeeding in school meant that one played the game, "survival in the institution," and won. The point that you make in the last sentence about locking children away from the world, how then can we expect them ever to be able to function in the world?

The idea that the school system is just an institution, of which the main goal is to insure its own survival and its profit rather than to educate children, is clearly stated by your second paragraph.

The example of the "Plan to Increase Student Happiness" that you used in your third paragraph is excellent. Between dumbing down, a fear of injuring self-esteem and the desire to pass the product along to the next person, some instructors might as well hand out "A" grades in the second week. I agree with you when you accuse people of using schools as day-care centers or pseudo-families. The purpose of schools is to teach children, not to baby-sit them, while the parents are working. I would like to know more about how much literacy decreased when compulsory schooling was first introduced.

The first sentence of your fourth paragraph contains a number of good points. I think some of these points are, indeed, good enough to deserve their own sentences. The fact that mass schooling puts so much emphasis on grades is disturbing. Children should be worried about learning, not about doing well in school. The latter is different from getting an education, as you keep pointing out. The idea that schools promote the belief that happiness can be bought is one with which I agree rather strongly with. One is constantly told throughout schooling that the purpose for becoming schooled is to obtain a high paying job. This implies that a high salaried job is they key to happiness. More often than not, such a job is the key to ulcers. Your last sentence in this paragraph, the idea that no one escapes from being schooled with his humanity intact, is particularly striking.

Your last paragraph is a fairly good conclusion. In it you mention most of the main points of your other paragraphs. I especially like the statement that schooling is mostly a waste of time and money. I wonder if anyone has done a study of how much money is wasted teaching children facts that they will not remember or need. It is my personal belief that everything that currently takes all of grade school to teach could be taught in two years or less. In the school I was in before I had to return to public school, we had just finished geometry in the sixth grade. In the public school geometry wasn't taught until high school. The class I got dumped into due to the fact that I had come from "outside" was just starting on the idea of negative numbers. That is a concept that I had already been taught three years before. Sorry, I got carried away there. I also like the point that you make that education is a living thing that applies everywhere, not just to what one has to do in school.

The purpose of your paper was to compare and contrast, as well as differentiate between education and schooling and through this comparison to illustrate how schooling is a vastly inferior substitute for education.

The paper was well written for an audience who, like myself, agrees with what you are saying. Someone who does not agree might, however, feel alienated by the idea that the schooling that they went through was a farce and therefore useless. The idea that someone is attacking the institution that one has spent a good deal of time in and which was apparently responsible for one's current position could be a mite upsetting. Your tone is one of disgust at the school system. Your arrangement might be changed so that all of the similar points were grouped together. You develop your ideas well if somewhat haphazardly. I liked the way that you kept using throughout the paper the catchy title and the phrase, "If only we were educated." As you know, I find your topic most INTERESTING!

Cheryl Lewis' Response to a Draft on Aging in Hemingway's Story "A Clean, Well-Lighted Place"

Linda, I feel the purpose of your paper is to explain why older people, in this story and in real life, are drawn to a clean, well-lighted place. The tone of the paper is descriptive and explanatory, and sympathetic to the sufferings of older people. You don't offer a solution; you just explain why older people are this way.

Your first paragraph is direct and to the point. It introduces the theme in a blunt style. I like it; it gets your point across.

Your second paragraph is very descriptive of the story. It is a good development paragraph. You lay the groundwork to build your following ideas on. The tone is descriptive and sympathetic.

The third paragraph continues with the description of the story, then goes into the problems the elderly face. It is a very good account of the things older people face. It explains why the old man acts the way he does. My only question is—is there any hope for these people? I realize it would put a totally different slant on your paper that you might not want. I just like to know that people have hope! I think that is why I don't like Hemingway's story—too depressing! I do like the way you explain it. It makes the old man a possible victim of aging and illness, not just a crazy old man.

The reference in the fourth paragraph to the National Institutes of Health is very effective. It drives home that these statistics are facts. The paragraph adds to the sympathetic tone toward the two old men in the story.

The fifth paragraph is basically informative. It also contrasts the young man to the older men. You are as understanding and sympathetic to the young man as you are to the old. You follow this through to the next paragraph. I like the use of the discussion between the two waiters. It develops the contrast between young and old, companionship and loneliness.

I love the way you compare Hemingway to the old man in the story. It is ironic that he ended up like one of his characters 30 years later! Maybe if he didn't write so many depressing stories, he wouldn't have been depressed! I like your next to the last sentence best. It pulls the theme of the story and the ending of Hemingway's life into one statement.

Good job, Linda. You have good development, good consistent tone throughout, and you keep it moving and interesting.

HIGHLIGHTS

LEARN TO GIVE HONEST, HELPFUL RESPONSES:
(DESCRIPTIVE AND INTERPRETIVE)
(READER-BASED AS WELL AS CRITERION-BASED)

YOUR RELATION TO THE PIECE
YOUR TRANSFORMATION TO INTENDED
AUDIENCE

VOICE (PERSONA) YOU PERCEIVE

WHAT THE PIECE SAYS WHOLE
YOUR EXPERIENCE OF THE PIECE WHOLE

WHAT THE PIECE SAYS IN EACH SECTION
YOUR EXPERIENCE OF EACH SECTION

WHAT STRIKES YOU AS ESPECIALLY EFFECTIVE

WHAT YOU WANT TO KNOW MORE ABOUT

PARTING THOUGHTS

9

Drafting

Presenting and Responding
at the Drafting Stage

Group Session #1—In Class and After Class

At the start of class when working drafts are due, place a copy on your instructor's desk (if requested) and join your group. Don't pass out copies to your group until after everyone has presented his/her draft aloud. After greetings and paper shuffling, the group leader reviews procedures for the session. The first order of business is for each of you to declare your personal intention for the session. "Today I intend to read my draft aloud more confidently, with no apologies or explanations. If I stop and make an excuse, please remind me." Or "I feel very emotional and vulnerable about my subject. If I get choked up, be patient and supportive, and I'll keep going no matter what." Or "I'm feeling very preoccupied today with something personal and may have trouble concentrating. I'll do my best to pay attention."

Reading Aloud

Presenting a draft orally, performing it, is essential in learning to involve your ear, whether as reader or writer. Everyone should be ready with pen and paper to make notes while listening. The leader selects someone to begin. When it's your turn, make no apologies or explanations. Let your draft stand on its own even if you

107

know it can be better. Read aloud at a natural pace. If you notice something you want to write yourself a note about, stop briefly, tell the group you're writing yourself a note, and write the note without telling the group what you've noticed. Resume reading. When you reach the end, stop without commenting. Allow five minutes for the group, including yourself, to write impressions of the piece.

Reading Copies, Writing Responses

After each group member has presented his or her draft and members have recorded their impressions for five minutes, only then is it time to pass out the copies. For the remainder of the time allotted, begin writing your spontaneous yet structured response to each draft. Completing each response is your main homework for the next class. Follow the guidelines and provide vivid "movies of your mind." Pretend that you're speaking directly to the writer and write quickly, intuitively, spontaneously, and honestly. You might want to think of the writing as a personal letter. Always begin by explaining your connection with the writer's intention: "Your intention is to demonstrate the value of doctor-assisted suicide for terminal patients who choose death rather than long suffering. As one who values life and empathizes with suffering, I have very mixed feelings. I can't say I agree with you or disagree, really. Your essay makes me think about this troubling issue in a non-threatening way, and I like that. The speaker of the essay seems sensitive to the reader's strong feelings. I like how you present your points with the goal of our being as humane as possible, which is hard."

Be aware of your own tendencies, especially tendencies to apply rigid criteria as judgments rather than to act as a sensitive, thoughtful reader reading. Be sure to include your initial impressions of the draft, written in the five minutes just after hearing it read aloud. If you were moved emotionally, say so sincerely. Likewise if you were confused or offended or whatever. In other words, include the main feelings and thoughts of your initial responses even if reading the draft has caused some of your responses to change. It's useful to say "When I first heard it, I felt confused because I didn't understand your purpose, but later when I read the draft again, it seemed clear from start to finish."

In order to describe and interpret the draft, you may have to reread your copy several times, seeking to grasp the intention, tone, structure, and manner of development. You may have to outline the draft in order to see how the parts relate to the whole. In doing so, realize that you're engaging in this process not only to help others improve their writing, but also to help you develop your reading and critical thinking as well as writing. You're learning to detect and discuss features of thought and language. In length your response should be 450–550 words. It's a fastwrite and, although it should be legible, it needn't be revised or corrected or neat in appearance. It may be handwritten or typed, whichever you prefer.

Remember to start with how you connect with the piece. After that, the order is flexible. Try to keep the flow natural and spontaneous while at the same time including all elements.

HEURISTIC for RESPONDING

YOUR RELATION TO THE PIECE

YOUR TRANSFORMATION TO INTENDED AUDIENCE

VOICE (PERSONA) YOU PERCEIVE

WHAT THE PIECE SAYS WHOLE
YOUR EXPERIENCE OF THE PIECE WHOLE

WHAT THE PIECE SAYS IN EACH SECTION
YOUR EXPERIENCE OF EACH SECTION

WHAT STRIKES YOU AS ESPECIALLY EFFECTIVE

WHAT YOU WANT TO KNOW MORE ABOUT

PARTING THOUGHTS

GROUP SESSION #1—DRAFTING STAGE

Leader	Convene the session.
	Remind each writer to give a copy to the instructor (if requested).
	Invite the raising of unsettled issues.
	Ochestrate resolution.
	Review procedures for the session.
	Call for each member's special intention for the session.
Member	Declare a special intention for the session.

(15 sec. each)

Leader	Designate the first presenter.
	During each presentation and follow-up, keep time and ensure that the writer and responders follow guidelines.
	Designate a timekeeper while you (the leader) respond.

Writer	Make no apologies or excuses.
	Read your draft aloud at normal pace.
	When finished make no comments.
Responder	Tune your ear to the writer's draft.
	While listening, make notes.
	When the writer finishes, make no comments aloud.
	Fastwrite your initial impressions.

(5 min.)

IF CONFLICT ARISES

Leader	Talk constructively with whoever appears aggressive in the conflict.
	Help restore civility.
Advocate	Talk constructively with whoever appears defensive in the conflict.
	Help restore civility.

AFTER ALL WRITERS HAVE READ ALOUD AND RESPONDERS HAVE WRITTEN IMPRESSIONS FOR ALL

Writer	Hand out copies of your draft.
Responder	Get a copy of each writer's draft.
	Study each copy as well as your notes and five-minute fastwrite of initial impressions.
	Fastwrite your response to each writer's draft (450–550 words).
	Bring your response to the next class.
Leader	Invite the members to raise unsettled issues.
	Orchestrate resolution.
	If necessary, consult your instructor.
	Close the session.

Group Session #2—In Class and After Class

Complete all of your responses before the start of the next class and bring them for distribution to each writer, but don't hand them out until after the oral session is concluded. (Your instructor may request a copy, too.) The group leader reviews procedures for the session. Each of you declares your personal intention. "I'm going to do my best not to act defensive as you respond to my work, no matter how defensive I may feel. I'm going to keep quiet and take notes." Or "I feel intimidated today because your papers always seem better than mine. I need to declare this feeling and ask for your support. Be honest but kind." Or "Mary, your draft touched me very deeply because I, too, lost a baby, and I feel threatened that we're going to be talking about that subject. I need for you two younger guys to try to understand how hard this has been for us. My intention is to assume that we're all in this together and we'll support each other while at the same time being honest about the writing."

Giving Oral Responses

The group leader determines which writer will be the first to receive oral responses. Take a few minutes to review your written response. One by one, each group member speaks his/her response, using the written response as a guide. Don't read the response verbatim. That's usually stilted and boring. Talk through it as naturally as you can. Make eye contact and address the writer directly. After three minutes the group leader will signal that time is up. Finish your sentence and stop. With practice you can learn to deliver a thorough response to a shorter paper within three minutes. Each member of the group does likewise, responding orally for about three minutes.

Thinking of what to say and saying it fully are important to your learning. It's fine to repeat what another has said if that's what you had in mind to say. If every responder states the main intention similarly or identifies a passage where s/he got confused, then the writer gets a clear indication of the main message coming across or of the need to clarify a passage. If all responders mention the same phrases as ones they especially like, then the writer gets a clear indication of what stands out as effective. While hearing each response, the writer listens quietly and makes notes. Sometimes one phrase said aloud by a responder will open the door to major revision. After everyone has finished giving and receiving oral responses, then members distribute their written responses to each writer.

Looking Toward Revision

For the rest of the allotted time, each writer studies his/her draft, notes, and the group's written responses, thinking about possible revisions needed to make a better draft. This can be a demanding task if you've received conflicting responses. Your job is to sort through the possibilities and then decide for yourself what you should do. Allow yourself time to think for yourself. If necessary, consult with your group or your instructor, but don't expect others to decide for you. They may help you review your options and send you away again to contemplate them on your own. In making your decisions, especially consider your audience and intention. Remember that your intention is to transform your audience in some particular way.

GROUP SESSION #2—DRAFTING STAGE

Leader	Convene the session.
	Remind each writer to give a copy to the instructor (if requested).
	Invite the raising of unsettled issues.
	Ochestrate resolution.
	Review procedures for the session.
	Remind members not to give the written response to the writer until after they've given all oral responses.
	Call for each member's special intention for the session.
Member	Declare a special intention for the session.

(15 sec. each)

Leader	Designate the first writer and order of the responders.
	Throughout the session, keep time and ensure that the writer and responders follow guidelines.
Writer	Tune your ear to each responder.
	Listen for cues to possible revision.
	Make notes throughout.
	Don't try to defend your writing.
	Keep quiet and listen throughout.
	When asked a question, don't answer it, but write it down for later thought.
	Say almost nothing except "Thank you."
Responder	Make no apologies or excuses.
	Address the writer directly.
	Make eye contact throughout, except when consulting your notes.
	Use your written response as a guide, but don't read it verbatim.
	Speak conversationally.
	In using the heuristic, describe, interpret, give "movies of the mind," offer "reader-based" as well as "criterion-based" responses.

(3 min.)

IF CONFLICT ARISES

Leader   Talk constructively with whoever appears
                aggressive in the conflict.
                Help restore civility.

Advocate   Talk constructively with whoever appears
                defensive in the conflict.
                Help restore civility.

AFTER ALL ORAL RESPONSES HAVE BEEN GIVEN FOR EVERY WRITER

Responder   Give your written response to each writer.

Writer   Collect written responses.

Leader   Invite the members to raise unsettled issues.
                Orchestrate resolution.
                If necessary, consult your instructor.
                Close the session.

Coaching Generative Responses

It's not easy learning to respond generatively, to help each writer look constructively toward composing a better draft. It's also not easy learning to coach one another in doing so. As your group begins the process, some members will undoubtedly feel self-conscious or inadequate or confused or overconfident— some stew of feelings that may hinder progress. When you sense such feelings in others, you may feel especially reluctant to coach them. They're already anxious, and you don't wish to hurt their feelings by intervening. If you do try to coach them, they may act defensive, too, which compounds tension. Two things need to happen. The group needs to discuss periodically the importance of coaching one another and of accepting coaching as a regular occurrence. And each member needs to agree to coach and be coached. Choir members during rehearsals expect the director to coach them until their parts are just so. Otherwise, they would sound mediocre when performing. Before I was born, my mother sang in the choir at St. Olaf College, one of the finest choirs in the nation. Imagine the quality and intensity of coaching they must have received as they prepared to tour and appear on special radio broadcasts nationwide. I remember hearing her perform solos for weddings and funerals when I was a little boy. She sang beautifully, with classical artistry, because she'd developed her inborn talent over years of coaching by first-rate teachers.

During a response session, while a responder is speaking, it's appropriate and necessary to interrupt politely and offer coaching. If the responder then acts defensive, which is bound to happen sometimes, then it's appropriate and necessary to offer coaching about his or her defensiveness. Although the leader may have primary responsibility for such coaching, groups function best when all members participate in coaching and being coached. Learning to employ the *heuristic* for responding at the drafting stage is comparable to learning how to solve a complex math problem. There's a procedure to guide you, but there's a whole lot of individual thinking and feeling required, too. And in a writing group there's the whole matter of social dynamics—four individuals interacting.

Where's the Professor?

When working drafts are first due, students put a copy on my desk as they walk in. They take their seats, and the leader convenes the group session. On this first day, students usually need little coaching from me about their group process. Some do need my coaching on their drafts. I sit at my desk fastreading each draft, considering just the elements we attend to at the drafting stage. I'm basically troubleshooting, looking for any draft that might need more help than I can fairly expect the group to provide. If a draft suits the assignment and seems pretty well focused, developed, and arranged, though perhaps rough, I put a check mark on the draft and in my grade book, indicating fulfillment of the requirement for composing and submitting a respectable working draft. This check also indicates my faith that any improvements needed can be accomplished by attentive group work and thoughtful rewriting.

If a draft doesn't suit the assignment or doesn't display adequate focus, development, and/or arrangement, I write notes to the writer suggesting areas that need attention. If the draft, despite its shortcomings, shows evidence of sufficient work by the writer, I put a check mark on it and in my grade book, indicating its fulfillment of the required work to date. If needed, I invite the writer to talk with me right after class or as soon as possible—in plenty of time to develop a good working draft before the next class meeting (as well as write responses to the three drafts of the other group members). I want to support the writer in catching up and adhering to the group's schedule. Near the end of the period, I hand back the drafts and talk with whoever needs to talk and make appointments for later conferences.

The next class period is quite different. Especially early in a term, groups usually need lots of my coaching as they respond orally. Although they review the written responses they've composed, many tend at first to read to the writer rather than speaking naturally. Some give advice—"you should do this; you should do that"—rather than primarily describing and interpreting the writer's draft, rather than giving "movies of the mind," rather than showing the writer how the draft affects and transforms them as an audience. Many are reluctant to coach one another in the procedures and nature of the work. So I sit down with a group for perhaps fifteen minutes, coaching, modeling, reinforcing, supporting their process. Then I move on to another group. I remind the class periodically not to feel dependent on me but to develop self-reliance and independence. If a group displays a rash of problems, I invite open conversation either during class or in privacy later.

HIGHLIGHTS

LEARN TO GIVE HONEST, HELPFUL RESPONSES:

(DESCRIPTIVE AND INTERPRETIVE)
(READER-BASED AS WELL AS CRITERION-BASED)

YOUR CONNECTION WITH THE PIECE
YOUR TRANSFORMATION TO INTENDED
AUDIENCE

WHAT THE PIECE SAYS WHOLE
YOUR EXPERIENCE OF THE PIECE WHOLE

WHAT THE PIECE SAYS IN EACH SECTION
YOUR EXPERIENCE OF EACH SECTION

WHAT STRIKES YOU AS ESPECIALLY EFFECTIVE

WHAT YOU WANT TO KNOW MORE ABOUT

PARTING THOUGHTS

ACCEPT THAT THIS WORK IS CHALLENGING AND
TAKES TIME TO LEARN

COACH ONE ANOTHER IN LEARNING TO
RESPOND AND INTERACT CONSTRUCTIVELY

SEEK HELP FROM YOUR INSTRUCTOR
YET CULTIVATE INDEPENDENCE

10

Smoothing Ruffled Feathers

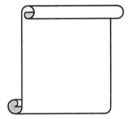

Writers Anonymous?

Odessa is a superior writer and knows it. She's self-conscious, though, about being the only African American in the group and wonders if race is an issue for anyone. Jack, a skilled carpenter who's working toward a degree in architecture, feels intimidated by her abilities and insecure about his own. But he's attracted to her and thinks about asking her to dinner even though she's eighteen and he's twenty-six. Jennifer doesn't like conflict and will do just about anything to keep the boat steady. She feels threatened by Odessa's direct criticisms of people's writing even though her insights seem remarkable. Jack's apologetic behavior about his writing doesn't bother her, but she feels impatient with his nonstop desire to talk about his fully restored, mint-condition 1969 Impala convertible—turquoise. Shing Po, a thirty-nine-year-old Asian American who operates a gourmet pizza cafe, respects the potential abilities of all three but sometimes makes Jane very uncomfortable when he complains about the failure of too many American students, his group included, to discipline themselves, prepare their work on time, and stay on task. He does feel self-conscious about his English even though he was born and raised in Virginia. When he was a child, his parents spoke mostly Vietnamese and sometimes French, but rarely English.

The group has selected Shing Po as leader. He's very good at orchestrating their work because he's organized, committed to excellence, experienced at managing people, and likes keeping on task. While serious, he has a delightful sense of humor, which helps promote joy in the work. He opens each session by asking if anyone has an issue to bring up before the work on writing begins. Jennifer feels flushed; she's anxious that someone will cause conflict. Then she remembers her troubling decision to speak to Jack about the car issue. Her throat feels tight, but her impatience has festered long enough.

"I have onc," she says. There's knee-jerk silence. Jennifer bringing up an issue? "Jack, you're a good student, and you contribute a lot to our group, but there's something I just have to say." Jack nods and waits. "I feel uncomfortable when you talk about your car. I know it means a lot to you. I know it's special, and I appreciate that. But when you talk about it in the group, I feel distracted from our work. It's not so much that you take up a lot of time, but I feel impatient, my feeling hangs on for awhile, and it's hard to think about the writing. I'd appreciate it if you wouldn't talk about it here. I'm working on the way I react, too, but I just had to say this."

"Thank you, Jennifer," Shing Po says kindly. "Jack, what do you want to say?"

"Look, I'm sorry, but I've been going through a lot with my divorce and all, and I don't need personal criticism here, too. My former wife hates it when I talked about my car. She said I care more about that car than about her. So—"

"Excuse me, Jack," interjects Shing Po. "We know you're going through a lot, and we support you. You know we do. Right now, Jennifer is expressing something that we can handle together calmly. She's not meaning to criticize you. She's being honest about her reaction to something that bothers her, and she's requesting your help with it. Please try to take it in that spirit."

Jennifer feels really bad now because she hurt Jack's feelings and wants to take back what she said. She and Jack have had coffee together a few times after class, he's confided in her, and she's very empathetic about the breakup of his marriage. She's normally the designated advocate in the group, but Odessa kindly steps in and says to her, while Shing Po talks quietly with Jack, "Jennifer, look, I know it seems like you hurt Jack's feelings, but he really needed to hear that. I've thought about saying it myself because it drives me crazy every time he brings up his car. It's like he's bragging or something to make up for his feeling of rejection. I don't know. I like him and empathize with him, too, but for the sake of the group and for his own sake in the future, he needs to hear that and learn to talk civilly about issues that affect our group. You didn't do anything wrong."

Jack appears calmer now, less defensive after his private talk with Shing Po. Getting Jennifer's attention, he says, "You're right, Jennifer, I do talk a lot about my car, and I appreciate your being honest with me about how it affects you. Do you want to go for a ride this afternoon with the top down? The sound system's great. Just kidding. I know I get defensive, and do the same thing when you're talking about my writing. It must be hard for you to respond to my writing when you just know I'll probably get upset. So today when you respond to my draft, I'm determined to shut up and listen, as Harrington says, no matter how defensive I may feel."

"Whew," Shing Po exclaims. "I'm glad that's over. Seriously, does everyone feel okay now? No unfinished business? Odessa?"

"Well, I for one want to compliment you, Jack, on your decision to work with us on this. Thanks."

"Thanks, but don't thank me yet. Wait and see if I bite your head off later, when you respond to my essay, which isn't very good."

"Shut up, Jack."

"I know. I know. Don't apologize for my writing."

You might be thinking this sounds like a self-help group, as one of my students quipped the other day. Actually, a good writing course is very much a self-help group—focused on composition. Traditionally, a self-help group is a voluntary gathering of people who believe they can learn to interact in such mutually purposeful ways that as individuals they achieve their main goal—ongoing sobriety, or weight control, or violence-free relationships. Although the brunt of many jokes, such groups enable millions of people to lead their lives as they choose rather than as victims of addiction or other dominant force. Because writing is such a demanding act, it brings us face to face with countless issues—intellectual, emotional, physical, spiritual, social, psychological. Many college students drop or fail composition because they feel unwilling or unable to face the requirements.

One common example, especially in conscientious students, is self-conscious insecurity about writing that can virtually paralyze a writer. Deafening voices from the past declare "not good enough, not good enough, not good enough." Blank paper remains blank. Or one imperfect opening sentence gets rewritten and discarded over and over and over. It's necessary for students to develop high standards and to strive for excellence, but in doing so, they must also develop healthy, productive work habits that enable them to meet deadlines and face the responses of others. The writing group, guided by the instructor, offers a vehicle for facing and resolving such challenges together. It's not a psychotherapy group—of course. But for it to work as a group, it must face and try to resolve the human issues that cause breakdowns in the writing or in the group as a group.

Developing as a writer doesn't mean simply producing writing that succeeds, although that's of course the main goal. It also means learning to overcome the forces that cause you to procrastinate, or to waste precious time because your methods are counterproductive, or to remain in ignorance about refining your style. A writing group is necessarily a self-help group, a voluntary gathering of people who believe they can learn to interact in such mutually purposeful ways that as individuals they achieve ongoing improvement in the quality of writing, methods of writing, and ability to collaborate about writing. The group functions best when focused intently and joyfully on the work at hand. Regular tune-ups ensure that nothing prevents smooth, dependable operation.

Regular Tune-ups

Our bicycles, cars, and other vehicles serve us only if we maintain them regularly. I was reminded of this last weekend while riding my mountain bike up Rockfish Gap to the Blue Ridge Parkway. Being fat and out of shape, I needed the lowest gear on the steepest climbs. As I tried to shift, the chain wouldn't lift all the way onto that largest rear sprocket. It would catch on a few teeth and then drop back onto the smaller sprocket. Why? That shifter usually glides like a bird. Because I'd neglected to check out my bike before the ride. It had seemed fine on my last ride in the fall. We make such bad assumptions less often about our vehicles than we do about our relationships.

Any valued relationship deserves and requires regular maintenance. Your writing group is a relationship that in many ways determines your success or failure in composition. When the group breaks down or spins its wheels or loses power, each member is affected adversely. Or at least each member misses the benefits of a group well tuned. Tuning a group, like tuning a bike, requires skill and practice. Mainly, it requires our attention to things at hand. On my bike ride, I thought I'd done everything I could to resolve my shifting problem. The shifting mechanism is pretty easy to adjust. I tightened the cable. No luck. I loosened the cable. No luck. So I finished my ride without the lowest gear and the next day took my bike to the shop. The mechanic immediately saw a small twig preventing the chain from sliding onto the largest rear sprocket—something I'd have noticed myself if I'd paid better attention. With your group, although your instructor will help, you learn to identify and solve problems together, on a regular basis, not just when a major breakdown occurs. Like Jennifer above, observe where your mind goes during group sessions. What within you or from someone else might be preventing you from working effectively?

Mature Conversation

Tuning a group requires mature conversation—honest but diplomatic expression of feelings, attitudes, and thoughts combined with respectful listening by all. No offense intended, but most of us experience too little of such conversation in our lives. Jack's defensiveness, above, results in part from the pain of his recent divorce. But it's also a personal characteristic that shows up elsewhere in his life as a hindrance to mature conversation. On the job, he's a fine timber-frame carpenter who takes pride in outstanding work. On the rare occasion when the boss or customer criticizes his work or finds a mistake, he falls into an emotional tailspin and tends to speak in a defensive-aggressive tone, which of course tends to perturb the boss or customer. He keeps on working, but he allows himself to feel miserable, not only because of the imperfection in his work but also because of his having spoken harshly to people who'd said what needed saying. Even if the boss or customer delivers the criticism without much appreciation for the usual fine work Jack provides, as though Jack were a shoddy carpenter, it's really Jack's inability to respond maturely in conversation about the work that undercuts his interactions and well-being.

To learn to write, Jack must learn to receive and use criticism of his writing virtually every class period. He must learn that criticism is a natural, necessary part of the writing process, just as the baseball coach's criticism had helped make Jack one of the best pitchers his high school will ever see. He must learn that mature conversation among adults, while difficult when about major issues, is not only possible but also essential for healthy relationships. A writing group practices the presentation of criticism in a constructive manner, which helps writers keep from becoming defensive. But even if a responder presents criticism harshly, it's the writer's responsibility to receive it willingly. It's also essential for group members, as Jennifer above, to bring up troubling issues before they fester. Too often in relationships, we go along day by day as though things are fine, not wanting to upset the order of things. Our feelings fester until they finally erupt, and then it's hard to express ourselves with maturity, and hard for others to hear us with civility.

Resolving Breakdowns in the Group as a Group

You choose your friends, but you don't usually get to choose your classmates or group members. One member may feel superior to the others as writers. Especially if that student's writing is actually superior, it's understandable that some attitude of superiority may have developed. We all have feelings and attitudes that work against our being good family members, friends, lovers, colleagues, or team members. An attitude of superiority is not in itself a concern of the group. But when the attitude shows up in behavior that undercuts the group, then the group must work to resolve the problem. It's hard to interact productively with an arrogant know-it-all who talks nonstop. Usually the problem is more subtle. The superior one pretends to listen to the responses of others, but doesn't really because, after all, what help can they possibly offer? It can be quite maddening to them when hard work and sincere effort fall on deaf ears. Similarly, the superior one may read others' drafts narrow-mindedly, as a know-it-all, as if there is but one superior way to think about an issue or construct an essay—"my way."

I choose this illustration because, while a can of worms, it's not so uncommon, and it has a revealing corollary. When in the presence of a superior writer, other students may feel inferior and intimidated. Believing themselves incapable of offering real help to the superior writer, they prevent themselves from learning to do so. Any writing, as any writer, can be improved. And even inferior writers can learn to help a superior writer. Odessa (above) knows this, and as a superior writer, she listens intently to what each responder says. Jennifer, Jack, and Shing Po sense her respect for them as honest—if less experienced—readers of her work, and they do their best to help her at every stage. She's very interested in developing herself as a writer, and she's grateful to them for the many ways they help her improve. Throughout high school she made straight A's, and now in college she's doing the same. She is indeed a superior academic writer, who does extensive research, thinks logically and insightfully, and writes with unusual clarity. However, she's learning that her style sometimes feels dry and impersonal, and she wants to enliven it, create memorable images, engage and hold the reader without compromising academic quality.

As honest, hardworking readers who follow the guidelines for each stage of the writing, Jennifer, Jack, and Shing Po help her do that. Jack has spent many years perfecting his special craft as a timber-frame carpenter, and he brings to their table the eye and ear of an artisan. Though just beginning his college education, he senses the deep tie between the composition of an essay and the construction of a fine timber-frame house. His observations about her writing—and about writing as a process—sometimes intrigue and excite Odessa. She is also having more fun working on writing than she used to, partly because Shing Po sees a place for humor and fun in nearly every serious matter, one reason his employees and customers in the pizza cafe appreciate him so much. We've already seen the conviction and courage—in the face of her insecurities—that help make Jennifer a strong group member. And of course each member has many other good qualities that I haven't mentioned.

Arrogance and Other Bugaboos

Most of us display a mix of good and not-so-good character traits. Whatever our makeup, although we may try to display our best behavior in various, especially public, situations, the rigors of college work and of interacting in a writing group are bound to unleash our not-so-good traits from time to time. Arrogance is but one example. An arrogant group member may require very special group intervention. Who's going to do it? When? How? Such is rarely easy, but often mature conversation—even if one sided—can promote self-awareness and improved behavior. People are human. Arrogant behavior is often a mask for insecurity or shyness. Bringing counterproductive behavior to light in a caring, constructive manner can relieve pressure on both sides and enable progress—but it ain't easy.

"Carmen, I've been feeling not very useful in responding to your writing because, even though I try hard to offer my honest observations, I notice that the next version doesn't seem to show any signs of revision generated by my observations. Your writing is good, as I've told you, but any writing can improve, and when I mention passages that feel unclear or incomplete, I'd appreciate your giving my observations more attention. Not that I'm right necessarily, but I get the feeling that my observations aren't really heard."

"I've been wanting to bring this up, too, Carmen. I've noticed the same thing about my responses. I don't feel heard either, and I must admit I've stopped trying very hard to see the places in your work that might be improved. I've got just so much time, and I don't like to feel like I'm wasting any. You're a much better writer than maybe I'll ever be, but I'm a pretty good reader, and I'd appreciate your respectful attention to my responses. I noticed that you got a B+ on your last essay—mainly because of stuff we'd brought up in the drafting stage and again in the refining stage. We do want to help you, you know, and it's frustrating that you don't seem to want us to."

"Well, you know this group stuff's not my idea of college work. Professor Harrington's a pro. He should be teaching us and not leaving it up to us. I mean on my last paper, for instance—I mean, I'd never gotten anything less than an A on any paper in my life. If he'd read my drafts and showed me what he wanted, then

I would've done it and gotten an A. I don't see why I should have to go through all these stages and stuff with people who don't know as much as I do about writing."

"Don't hold back, Carmen."

"Seriously, I feel like I'm wasting my time in this group stuff. I want to do my papers, get my grades, and get out of this lame course. I don't see why I have to take it anyway. I made all A's in high school, and I'm going to make all A's in college. I've already rewritten that last paper and turned it back in to Harrington. I'll bet it's an A."

"It might have gotten an A the first time if you'd considered respectfully what we said in our responses and made thoughtful revisions instead of being bullheaded about your own way."

"Hey, no name calling, Mark. Keep to the guidelines."

"Sorry, but I'm frustrated, and you do seem bullheaded, Carmen."

"Mark."

"Okay. Okay. Sorry, Carmen. No more name calling. But please listen to us or I'm going to talk with Harrington about getting in a different group."

"Threats aren't constructive either, Mark."

"Okay. Okay. But I'm serious. I'm also frustrated because I don't feel you hear or read my papers carefully either, Carmen. It's like you can't allow yourself to acknowledge that there might be another point of view that's just as valid but very different from yours. I need each group member to respond respectfully from a spirit of openness and generosity, like Harrington said, not just from one view. Our purpose in writing an essay isn't to be right, although we all seek the truth, but to be a reasonable, credible, sincere exploration of an idea. To do that, we need readers who are supportive, open, thoughtful, and critical only in the best sense."

"I sort of get what you mean, Mark. I guess I didn't hear Harrington either when he talked about that—about the main purpose of our essays. My dad's a demanding son-of-a—you know—well, you don't know—but he is—sorry about my language—and I'm pretty uptight about grades and all. I guess I come across as pretty much of a know-it-all. I feel pretty wound up most of the time. So—I'm very skeptical about this group stuff. I've always been pretty much of a loner. Maybe we should get Harrington over here."

"Well, we can do that if you want, Carmen, or we can try to work things out ourselves. What do you think, Mark?"

"Well, I'm willing to try to work things out ourselves. I mean we've got to stop depending so much on our teachers and learn to take responsibility ourselves. What do you think, Franz? By the way, what kind of name is that, Franz—Dutch?"

"German. My mother was born in Heidelberg and met my father when he was there as an exchange student. She decided to go to college in the States so she could be with him, and she just stayed here. Anyway, I think we should try to work things out and see how it goes, but I'm frustrated with how things have been going. What do you say, Carmen?"

"Well, Franz, I've noticed that your responses to me have seemed lackadaisical—like you're not trying. I get what you said about my not listening well to you or anyone in the group for that matter. You know, it's not personal. You guys are fine.

My beef is with the way the course is set up. So I guess I need to talk with Harrington myself and see what he says."

"Do you have a problem with being the only girl, I mean woman, in the group, Carmen?

"I don't think so. I mean what does gender have to do with it? I'll think about it. No, I think I just need to talk with Harrington and see if we can work things out. I'll see him right after class and let you know what happens."

"Would you rather talk with him as a group?"

"No, I don't think so. I'd rather do it by myself. I know he wants everyone to be satisfied with how their writing improves. So, thanks for talking with me about things. I'll get back to you."

"Good. Thanks for listening."

In this scenario, the group talks maturely about a very sensitive personal issue, Carmen's pesky behavior. While such challenging conversation must be initiated as needed, it's also essential for the group to understand that, although Carmen's behavior seems annoying and counterproductive, the others are responsible for their reactions to it. Carmen's behavior contributes to the breakdown, and so does everyone else's. My wife Victoria, a psychotherapist, explained to me that the family of an alcoholic tends to blame the alcoholic for its many problems. When the alcoholic quits drinking, leaves by divorce, or dies, virtually all of the same problems, except one, continue to plague the family. In fact, the family then usually starts blaming its problems on another member. Two of the most challenging human qualities to develop are self-awareness and self-possession. It's easier to blame others than to take responsibility ourselves for our own behavior.

Breakdown—You're Absent or Unprepared

Other kinds of breakdowns happen, too, such as being absent or unprepared—for whatever reasons. When they do, learn to deal with them constructively. What matters is integrity and responsibility in carrying on the work of the course or, as occasionally happens because of personal circumstances, deciding to withdraw. People who are engaged in ongoing communication about their work and their work relationships are better prepared to deal constructively with such breakdowns. Those experiencing the breakdown are more likely to acknowledge it honestly, and the others are more likely to respond with support, flexibility, and ideas for solution.

If you must be absent, phone your partner, preferably before the session, and arrange for another call following the session to discuss the makeup. (If you can't reach your partner or another group member, phone the instructor.) Your partner can then inform the group as well as the instructor both of your absence and of your intention to arrange things. Such intentions in themselves can make a great difference in how things turn out. If you're unprepared and considering being absent because of, say, embarrassment, I urge you to take part anyway, unless your instructor (like one of my colleagues) requires that you not participate if unprepared. You contribute to others both by participating and by acknowledging honestly your unpreparedness. They contribute to you by accepting your participation and by supporting you in navigating rough waters.

If you're often absent or unprepared, that's another, more serious sort of matter to face—for your group and especially for you. When you examine yourself in the mirror, what do you see? Family responsibilities such as an ailing father or child? Money problems? Poor academic preparation for college? Fear of failure? Procrastination? Academic laziness? In the fall of 1959, at the young age of seventeen, I enrolled as a freshman at Duke University. I'd gone to a fine prep school for boys in grades 7–9, where everyone studied Latin as well as a modern foreign language, along with the usual run of subjects. All tests were essay tests, and we wrote papers in more classes than just English. After all that, high school had seemed pretty easy. Although my high school had been respectable, I'd not had to study very hard or long to make A's and be invited into the National Honor Society. Duke was another story. The standards and competition were fierce in every class. It seemed like every student had been all-state this and all-American that. I attended classes religiously and took such good notes that my friends often borrowed them—but I didn't study regularly in any real sense of the word. Plenty of my friends studied at least eight hours a day, six or seven days a week, in addition to classes and labs. Me, I played roofball, frisbee, and a host of other typical college games, and I swilled beer with the best—or worst. I crammed for tests and wrote my papers at the last minute.

I must say I was happy to be on my own, away from strict, demanding parents. But in retrospect I realize—and I admit to you now—that I was unconsciously intimidated by all that academic and athletic talent on the Duke campus. I was afraid, unconsciously, that if I tried and failed, I would prove my unworthiness to be there. So I didn't try. I sort of pretended to try, and I cultivated an image of myself as a fun-loving "college" boy. I never made a high-enough average to pledge Phi Kappa Psi, but the brothers invited me to live in their house anyway, against the rules, because I was available for a good time. Eventually I flunked out, as we say, and then had to spend several years working a job, going to night school, and studying during the wee hours to redeem myself academically and pay my dues before going on for my Master's and Ph.D. in English.

Nearly forty years later, I haven't forgotten my experience, my feelings, and the self-awareness I developed later. I can say honestly, I understand what can happen to a college student, even one who means well. I meant well. I longed to do better, but I just couldn't muster the gumption. If anything like this happens for you, do what I didn't do: Seek help. You may be pleasantly surprised how understanding a professor can be—if you level with her or him and not pretend that everything is okay when it isn't. You needn't bare your soul. You needn't explain your private business. But do take responsibility for your problem with those professors, department chairs, deans, and counselors whose life's work is the education of students. Together, perhaps you can negotiate a plan for your success in the course. Or if necessary and appropriate, perhaps you can achieve mutual understanding about the F grade your work deserves or make a clean break in dropping the course. Understand the value of walking away with your self-respect intact.

Tense situations occur daily in most relationships, households, work places, and wherever else humans find themselves being human. The point is to develop civilized, mature means for resolving tension and moving on. Like death and taxes, such barriers and their solutions are a natural part of life.

Professors Are Human, Too

It's not just students' feathers that get ruffled and need smoothing from time to time. Teaching is a demanding profession in any discipline. Orchestrating writing groups can be especially demanding because so much goes on at once, drawing the instructor's attention and expertise in many directions. I do my best to attend to each group with sensitivity and skill. Most groups learn to function well, no matter how diverse the members. But in nearly every class there's usually at least one group that needs special attention. One member is chronically unprepared for sessions and doesn't take responsibility for addressing the problem. Another member socializes too much and distracts the group from the work. The two other members may want to address the problem but feel reluctant to squeal to the instructor.

It's usually pretty easy for the instructor to notice that a certain group is having such problems. But not always. I urge you as a group member to do whatever it takes to improve your situation. Dare to address the group if necessary. If that fails, dare to speak to your instructor. Taking such responsibility requires courage, but it can help immensely. The instructor has experience and skill in addressing such problems. Still, being human, s/he may or may not be able to find a solution that suits everyone. I feel frustrated sometimes when a student is chronically unprepared and not addressing the issue openly, as though everything is okay. Many college teachers, while doing their best to foster student success, recognize a student's right to fail. There, a student's failure might not have much effect on the success of others. In a course involving group work, however, a student's ongoing failure can affect the work of at least three others.

I try to channel my frustration constructively and orchestrate resolution. Sometimes a group and I must settle for less-than-ideal results because we're all human. One of my greatest challenges as a writing teacher is accepting that, no matter how hard I work to improve my methods, a few students will probably fail to perform responsibly. Whatever shoes you fill, help your instructor resolve the many issues s/he must address in trying to make your class the best it can be. Try to work things out—TOGETHER—and recognize that s/he can't perform miracles, especially alone.

HIGHLIGHTS

DEVELOP TRUST IN THE MEMBERS OF
YOUR GROUP

PRACTICE MATURE CONVERSATION

ADDRESS A PROBLEM BEFORE IT FESTERS

GIVE AND TAKE CRITICISM WITH GOOD SPIRIT

TAKE RESPONSIBILITY FOR YOUR OWN FEELINGS
AND BEHAVIOR

CONSULT YOUR INSTRUCTOR AS NEEDED

IF YOU MUST DROP OR FAIL THE COURSE,
TALK HELPFULLY WITH YOUR INSTRUCTOR
AND GROUP

DARE TO PRESERVE YOUR SELF-RESPECT

REMEMBER THAT YOUR INSTRUCTOR
IS HUMAN, TOO

11

Refining
Learning to Refine Style

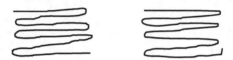

Fine Tuning

Refining style is fine tuning. You accomplish it mainly with your ear. Good writing engages readers and pleases them aesthetically. It's like music. The notes work together to create one purposeful effect. You've explored, drafted, and redrafted. You've solidified a good working draft so that all the major parts work together to create the desired whole. Now in the refining stage it's time to fine tune each paragraph within the whole. Granted, you've been tuning consciously and unconsciously all along. But your attention has remained focused primarily on the "big picture." In fine tuning, you bring into harmony the features of your own writing style. The problem is, it's hard to distinguish your own style. It's much easier to distinguish and describe someone else's—and even that takes practice.

Writing style is the character of the writing—the presence of the individual writer's being and language at work on the page. As with music, you can learn to experience distinctive features in the writing of each individual writer, including yourself. Imagine the possibilities in your group. I'm sure you've had the experience of being with a friend who notices musical elements you've overlooked. You might think you're really hearing a song on your favorite CD because you're so enjoying the words and melody and beat. Then your friend says, "What a great bass line," and you begin to hear and appreciate the bass as well. In this same way your group can help one another hear the music of everyone's writing.

Because I've listened to southern fiddle music for many years, at fiddler's conventions I can recognize from a distance the unique fiddling style of many particular fiddlers, just as I recognize many people's voices on the phone. People tell me that I have a unique fiddling style. But it's been harder for me to grasp the features of my own style, I guess because it feels natural. By paying attention to what people tell me about it and by listening to it more consciously, I'm learning to hear its features and thus discover ways to refine it.

WRITER
Refine style
Record draft on tape;
 listen back and refine
Run style-check

CONCERNS
Strategies for Refining
Opening
Rhythm and flow
Diction and imagery
Transitions
Closing
Format

Style(s)

Actually, we use a range of styles, just as we use a range of voices, each one cultivated to fit the purpose and audience. In much college writing, you want to develop a respectable academic style tailored to the discipline you're working in. Your history style becomes slightly different from your biology style. Even for the same course or discipline, you might compose papers that sound different. For composition class, you might develop one style to argue the benefits of home schooling, and another style to narrate a memorable personal experience. A research scientist uses a highly specialized style for the specialized readers of a science journal; a less-specialized style for the nonspecialized but knowledgeable readers of a popular science magazine; an even less-specialized style for the general readers of a weekly news magazine; and a personal style for her son in a letter.

We make many stylistic choices automatically, just as we do in speaking to different people with whom we have different relationships. Nearly automatically, we speak in one style to a certain close friend and in another style to a highway patrol officer who stops us on the interstate. You can see that style and voice are very closely related. Some would say they're the same. The matter of what style(s) and voice(s) a student should cultivate is complex. Various English departments and professors, not to mention professors in other disciplines, view the matter differently. Some of my own colleagues in English, for example, believe that composition courses should help students develop their range of styles and voices from personal to academic. Others believe that composition courses should cultivate just academic voices and styles. Your professor will help you and your classmates understand the expectations for your course.

Preparing for a Group Session at the Refining Stage

Before the refining session with your group, read your draft aloud to yourself several times, paragraph by paragraph. The first step in fine tuning your writing is trying to hear the music already playing—the images, sounds, and rhythms that create your intended effect in your own unique style. Hearing the music, you can also hear notes that squawk. Whenever you feel something nag at you, write a notation in the margin. Just a squiggly line will do. You can't always tell what's causing the squawk. Perhaps it's a choppy rhythm. Perhaps a phrase just doesn't sound right. Or perhaps you feel a jolting gap between paragraphs. Whenever you can, revise that passage until it does feel better. Writers usually try out different ways on paper or the word processor until they find one that seems to work. If you can't sense what to do with a passage, mark it in the margin and let it be. Something will probably occur to you later, just as someone's name pops into your mind a few hours or days after you couldn't remember it. Plus, your group will have plenty to offer. Members will hear squawks that to you sounded like music and will help prepare you to revise further.

Using a Cassette Recorder

I recommend using a cassette recorder to help train your ear. Record yourself reading your paper aloud at a slow but natural pace. Then while listening to it play back, follow along with your eyes. This technique enables greater auditory and visual concentration on the text. Your attention no longer needs to be divided between reading aloud, seeing, and listening—all of which take brain power. If you haven't tried this before, you'll be surprised at how many elements you notice about your writing—the music as well as wordiness, inappropriate choppiness, cumbersome sentence structure, a vague transition, unintended repetition, or an image that doesn't fit your intended meaning. Training yourself and practicing for a few weeks or months with the recorder will improve your ability to fine tune without the machine. Also, the more ably you refine your piece before bringing it to your group, the more they can focus on elements you simply can't detect yourself.

Using Your Writing Handbook

Your writing handbook includes sections on basic elements that affect style. Familiarize yourself with them to help focus your awareness. Notice how clichés common in our daily speech can make writing dead or trite. Pursue fresh language. Notice how wordiness, like debris, detracts from key words. Pursue conciseness and directness. Use the shortest word that works. Seek vividness, too. In your reader's mind create picturesque images. As to rhythm, let the flow of sentences reflect your meaning—at times short, crisp, intense—at other times smooth and languid like the Loire River at dawn. Notice how sexist language conveys gender inequity. Use considerate alternatives—unless you want to annoy some readers and make a special point about gender. Notice how an opening too general creates reader impatience. Embody your point specifically. Notice how a closing that merely summarizes creates anticlimax. Stimulate reader reflection on your point.

Good style is also a mystery. It's the magical sum of the writer's best self selecting the best possible language for the purpose. It can't be captured in mere guidelines. Such guidelines, though, as in your writing handbook, help build your awareness of possibilities. They help you detect music and squawks in your own writing and in the writing of your peers.

Presenting and Interacting at the Refining Stage

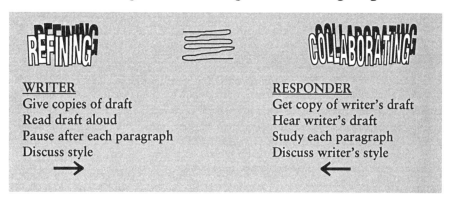

WRITER
Give copies of draft
Read draft aloud
Pause after each paragraph
Discuss style
→

RESPONDER
Get copy of writer's draft
Hear writer's draft
Study each paragraph
Discuss writer's style
←

The trick for the group is to open the door to possibilities for improving the writing without doing the writer's work. Ultimately you as the writer must sort through the group's responses and suggestions, struggle with your text, and make each stylistic decision on your own. Even after you've seen new possibilities, you must try them out, play with them, and read and reread until each passage feels right.

As usual, the group leader convenes the session, reminds members to submit a copy to the instructor if requested, and reviews procedures. Each member declares a special intention. The leader announces the length of time available for work on each draft and selects the first presenter, who passes out copies of his or her refined draft. Group members, including the writer, read the draft silently. Without apology or explanation, the writer reads aloud the title and pauses for comments. Anyone who wants to speak does so, and the writer makes notes. Then the writer reads the opening paragraph and pauses. Anyone who detects a stylistic matter to bring up does so. During the ensuing interaction, the writer mainly listens and writes notes, realizing that the job of rewriting comes later, alone. Groups usually waste time if they try to rewrite a sentence or passage to suit everyone. No offense to camels, but there's an old saying that "a camel is a horse designed by a committee." The writer decides later how and what appears on the paper. When the group feels satisfied with discussion of the first paragraph, the writer reads aloud the next one and pauses.

Again, any member who detects a stylistic concern brings it up. And so forth until the allotted time is up for that writer's draft. Later—alone—the writer can apply to the rest of the piece what s/he has learned in the discussion of some paragraphs. It's fair and practical to divide the refining time equally among all group members.

GROUP SESSION—REFINING STAGE

Leader	Convene the session.
	Remind each writer to give a copy to the instructor (if requested).
	Invite the raising of unsettled issues.
	Ochestrate resolution.
	Review procedures for the session.
	Call for each member's special intention for the session.
	Announce the time alotted for each writer's draft.
Member	Declare a special intention for the session.
	(15 sec. each)
Leader	Designate the first presenter.
	Keep time and ensure that the writer and responders follow guidelines.
	Designate a timekeeper when you (the leader) present your draft.
Writer	Give copies to the group.
Responder	Read the writer's draft silently without comment.
Writer	Read your own draft silently without comment.
Writer	Make no apologies or excuses.
	Read your title aloud and pause for comments.
	Read your first paragraph aloud and pause for comments.
	Mainly listen and write notes.
	Read your next paragraph aloud and pause for comments.
	And so forth through your paper.
	When time is up, thank the group.
Responder	Tune your ear to the writer's draft and developing style.
	While listening, make notes.

Responder	When the writer pauses, bring up any stylistic squawk you detect.
	If you have a suggestion, make it, but don't spend much time rewriting.
	Help the writer detect inconsistencies and shortcomings in his or her style.
	Avoid imposing your own style, though do help the writer understand the conventions of academic writing.

IF CONFLICT ARISES

Leader	Talk constructively with whoever appears aggressive in the conflict.
	Help restore civility.
Advocate	Talk constructively with whoever appears defensive in the conflict.
	Help restore civility.

Leader	Invite the raising of unsettled issues.
	Orchestrate resolution.
	If necessary, consult your instructor.
	Close the session.
Writer	Further refine your draft before the next group session.

Refining: A Scenario

Althea (Leader): "Morning, troops. Another day in the trenches. Hey, Juan, how's your mother doing? Is she home from the hospital?"

Juan: "Yeah, thanks. She's fine. It turned out to be routine appendicitis. She did the wash yesterday, believe it or not. My old Mom."

Mary: "We're glad to hear it."

Maj-Britt: "Yeah, it sounded serious before."

Juan: "Well, you can imagine we were all worried about her."

Althea: "For sure. Well, today, we're refining style, and Harrington said he's not taking any time for a mini-lesson, so we've got the whole period. Remember, we'll divide the time equally. You read your title and pause for comments. Then you read your opening paragraph and pause for comments. And so forth through the paper, one paragraph at a time. The writer mainly listens and takes notes. Mary, what's your special intention today?"

Mary: "Well, I sometimes hold back because I'm not confident about style matters, so today I'm determined to blurt out whatever I notice."

Althea: "Juan?"

Juan: "Today I'm not going to get defensive no matter how cruel and wrong you all are. Just kidding. I hate it when I get defensive, and I'm sure you don't much care for it either."

Maj-Britt: "I sometimes hold back because I don't want to hurt anyone's feelings. So today I'm determined to speak out about your writing even if it feels uncomfortable."

Althea: "As your noble leader, I sometimes let things go on too long. I'm going to keep to the guidelines and insist that you do the same. Okay? Then let's get started. Let's see, we have twelve minutes for each draft. Maj-Britt, how about if you start."

Maj-Britt: "Here are your copies."

Althea: "Let's read silently and quickly." [They read.]

Althea: "Okay, Maj-Britt."

Maj-Britt: *John Red Elk: Medicine Chief.*

Mary: "I like it as a title because it captures who he is really."

Juan: "I see what you mean, but the piece isn't mainly about the man but about Maj-Britt's encounter with him and what it means to her. It's about star-crossed love and spiritual growth. Shouldn't the title reflect the main theme?"

Mary: "Oh, I see. Yeah."

Althea: "How about 'Sleeping with the Enemy'?"

Maj-Britt: "Very funny, Althea. But I get the idea. I'll work on it."

Maj-Britt: *"I am man first. I am chief. I am warrior. I have earned my power. I take what I want. No man tells me what to do!" This was the passionate response of John Red Elk as he recounted the decision of his elders regarding his marriage to me. "No," they had said. "We forbid it." And then—much more gently—this strange mysterious man began talking of giving up his medicine, passing it on to another and living a quiet life with me. Sadness overshadowed his once powerful voice for he knew he could never leave his destined way. My heart and my spirit ached for him as he continued to talk of this peaceful and quiet life—this refuge—apart from his medicine.*

Juan: "Didn't your heart ache for yourself, too, because you and John were destined to split?"

Maj-Britt: "Oh, yeah. My heart was pounding. But I'm not sure I want to say so in that passage."

Althea: "I wonder if you might add *with me* into the last sentence to clarify that *this peaceful and quiet life* would be life with you as a married couple."

Mary: "Is it okay to start that sentence with *And*? My teachers always said never start a sentence with *And*.'"

Althea: "Is that a style issue or a proofreading issue? Anyway, it seems fine in this sort of piece. It's not strictly academic. You know what I mean?"

Juan: "I'll raise my hand and call Harrington over. [I join them.] Professor Harrington, can Maj-Britt start this sentence with *And*?"

Harrington: "It seems fine to me in this kind of narrative and reflective writing. It seems to work well with the rhythm. Yet it's a hard call to make, because it depends on the audience. When writing for a teacher or prospective employer, for example, it's usually best to avoid choices that might call attention to themselves. For me as your reader, it's fine here, in this kind of piece. Also, I see such sentences more and more, even in professional journals. Some of the old 'rules' don't apply in the same ways they used to."

Maj-Britt: "Okay, thanks. I'll look at it again."

Juan: "I love the rhythm of the opening—the short, intensive sentences depicting his anger and disappointment and then the smoother, softer rhythm depicting his relationship with you. The rhythm seems really expressive and appropriate throughout. Great."

Mary: "I agree. And I especially like *overshadowed* and *refuge* and *his destined way.* Anything else to bring up about this paragraph? No?"

Althea: "Yes, one more. It's a matter of rhythm and wordiness. In the last sentence you might say *talked* instead of *continued to talk.* Also, you might delete the second *my* and *and*? It would read, *My heart and spirit ached for him as he talked of this peaceful, quiet life—this refuge—apart from his medicine.*"

Juan: "Hey, how does it sound like this? *My heart and spirit ached as he talked of this peaceful life—this refuge from his medicine.* *Quiet* seems a lot like *peaceful,* and peaceful kind of interplays with the notion of peace pipe that would normally be part of his medicine back with the tribe. The rhythm sounds better this way, too. Good job, Althea."

Maj-Britt: "It is much better. Thanks. And deleting *for him* takes care of the issue Juan brought up before. All right. Thanks. I like it."

Althea: "Okay. Next paragraph?"

Where's the Teacher?

While my students work together at the refining stage, I either sit at my desk alert for a raised hand or visit each group for a few minutes, observing and coaching. When a hand pops up, I hurry over to help resolve the issue raised, such as whether a series of short, choppy sentences seems effective for the writer's purpose in that paragraph. Or group members might express concern that they're spending all of the writer's designated time on just one paragraph. Many such issues arise, and I take them up as efficiently and helpfully as I can. While sitting in with a group to observe and coach, I often detect stylistic matters that the students haven't noticed. Because style is so complex and in some ways individual, I find my students learn best from me in such specific situations than in a preplanned demonstration for the whole class. Occasionally, I'll stand up from sitting with a group, interrupt the whole class, and make a point for all. Sometimes after silently observing a group for ten minutes and seeing that they're doing fine without me, I simply compliment them and move on.

Continuing to Refine

Working together, with your instructor's coaching, your group can develop considerable awareness of your own and one another's styles—both the music and the squawks. Remember, it's in the struggle to hear the difference—and to transform the squawks into music—where the real learning takes place. You can imagine, I'm sure, the squawking I've had to transform in my fiddling.

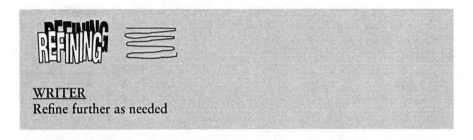

WRITER
Refine further as needed

After a refining session, you study your notes, apply what you've learned, and further refine your text as skillfully as you can. Perhaps you need mainly to clarify and smooth out the transitions between paragraphs. Or perhaps you need to rewrite passages where responders detected ineffective shifts in tone. Then you set about proofreading in preparation for the upcoming proofing session. A writer's work seems never done, right?

HIGHLIGHTS

DEVELOP THE HABIT OF FINE TUNING WITH YOUR EAR AND EYE

READ AND REREAD ALOUD

USE A CASSETTE RECORDER

USE YOUR WRITING HANDBOOK

LEARN TO DETECT MUSIC AND SQUAWKS

LEARN TO GRASP THE DEVELOPING STYLE OF EACH GROUP MEMBER, INCLUDING YOURSELF

INVITE COACHING

LISTEN AND MAKE NOTES

MAKE STYLISTIC DECISIONS YOURSELF

STRUGGLE TOWARD REFINEMENT

12

Proofing
Learning to Detect Annoyances

Annoying Readers?

Proofreading (or proofing) is the skill of seeing and correcting "errors" in a manuscript. Just before an article or book goes to press, an editor and usually the author examine a "proof" copy called the "proofs." They mark "errors" with proofreader's marks and/or make corrections so the published text will be "error" free.

Readers tend to be distracted and even annoyed by textual "errors." In a letter of application for a job, just one or two misspelled words will sometimes annoy the prospective employer so much that s/he'll reject the applicant, regardless of other qualifications. People tend to see "errors" as signs of illiteracy or laziness or disrespect.

College students are expected to learn in first-year writing how to see and correct such "errors." It's not uncommon for a professor of history or biology to remark, upon finding "errors" in an essay test or report, "Didn't this student learn anything in freshman composition?" People tend to judge writers by the surface "errors" of their texts, regardless of other important qualities in the writing.

However unfair such judgments may sound, they occur often and will continue to occur. It's much easier to learn to correct textual "errors" than to change how the world reacts to them. Fortunately, by means of collaboration and the stages of writing, it's now possible for student papers to be proofed so well that they're virtually free of "errors" when submitted to the instructor as "finished." It's also possible for students to internalize the proofing process and to apply it well even when under the stress of an essay exam in psychology or philosophy. Like the other matters of composition, proofing takes plenty of attention and practice.

WRITER
Proof and correct text
Record draft on tape;
  listen while proofing
Run spell-check
Run grammar-check

CONCERNS
Strategies for Proofing
Grammar
Usage
Punctuation
Mechanics
Documentation
Format

"Errors" and Expectations

Your instructor is usually the ultimate judge of your textual "errors," so you'll want to understand and act upon his or her expectations regarding proofreading. As usual, anticipate expectations regarding the quality of writing, the methods of writing, and the methods of collaboration. Set your goals accordingly:

❖ Turn in papers that are virtually free of "errors."

❖ Develop methods of proofing that will continue to work for you in your education, employment, and personal life.

❖ Help others learn to proof, and accept their help in your own learning.

These goals may seem like a tall order, especially if you think you're "poor in grammar," as many of my students say. An intriguing phenomenon for me as a writing teacher is that, after just a few weeks of attending to their writing as never before, most of my students improve their proofreading by leaps and bounds. So can you.

Natural Language

You know much more about language than you probably realize. Unless you've been immersed in collaboration and the stages of writing, you may not have learned to apply your tacit knowledge—your natural, unconscious knowledge—of oral and written language. When you get involved in writing and rewriting about subjects that matter, with readers who care about you and your writing, you pay closer attention. You discover ways to make your texts "look good" so readers will attend to your message. You notice more surface details of written texts, ask more questions, and look up more things—in the dictionary, thesaurus, writing handbook, and other resources.

With the help of your instructor and your group, you notice more of the patterns of "error" that are unique to you, and you learn ways to correct them. Although "school grammar" can be interesting and useful to learn, the systematic study of grammar does not in itself guarantee improvement in writing or even proofreading. Those abilities are learned primarily by doing them. You wouldn't expect to be able to play tennis simply because you can name the parts of a racket, specify the dimensions of a standard court, and recite the basic rules. Still, many Americans assume that the main way to improve writing and proofreading is to study grammar systematically. Don't expect your college instructor to spend much time on grammar as such. The majority of class time will be spent writing and discussing writing, including the craft of proofreading to correct surface "errors."

Appropriate Choices

I put "errors" in quotation marks because often it's not so much a matter of "errors" as inappropriate choices for the intended audience. An "error" in one piece may create a superb effect in another. Consider the opening of Mark Twain's novel *Huckleberry Finn*, brilliantly narrated as if in Huck's own words: "You don't know about me, without you have read a book by the name of 'Tom Sawyer,' but that ain't no matter." Imagine how it would flop if it said, "You, dear reader, know nothing about my humble person or circumstances unless of course you have read the novelistic endeavor *Tom Sawyer*, but for the present time such is of no consequence." Collaboration with your group and instructor reveals how intended readers actually do react—something you can't usually learn except by reading others' work and having them read yours. Especially important is learning to understand the rigorous expectations of academic readers and hence other professional readers.

When writing and rewriting, we make hundreds of choices, mostly unconsciously and naturally. In the proofing stage, the goal of proofreading is to notice and think about the choices we've made and then, if appropriate, make different choices for the finished text. Such choices determine the reader's access to the message of the writing:

it's / its	you are / you're
is / are	, / ; / .
alright / all right	alot / a lot
brazil / Brazil	accept / except

Inappropriate choices pull the reader's attention away from the writer's message, toward judgements about the writer, as with the employer and professors above. So you must think carefully about such choices; they do affect the quality of writing because they affect the reading process.

Proofing Alone

For the student writer, there are choices even more fundamental, having to do with habits, attitudes, and methods. The first is the choice whether or not to proofread. Many first-year students in college don't bother to proof, except perhaps hastily and superficially. This may seem odd, given readers' negative reactions to "errors," but it's very common.

This failure to proofread usually derives from a poor fit of the student's goals or planning and the teacher's expectations. A paper is usually due at a certain time. The instructor expects many hours of exploring, drafting, redrafting, editing, and proofing. Sometimes it takes longer than expected. Other things get in the way, such as a big test in economics. Students run out of time, barely get the final copy typed up, much less proofed, and turn it in at the last minute.

Another common possibility is that students proofread the final copy and find "errors" but because they don't want to mess up the neatly typed copy, they don't correct them. Traditionally, college teachers prefer to see last-moment corrections made neatly with a pen than to have to mark errors. I've met few college-writing teachers who prefer neatness to "correctness." Besides, nowadays word processing makes the correcting process easy.

Or perhaps students just get "sick" of working on a piece and turn it in to get rid of it. Last week while I was working with a college-prep student on "errors," she admitted she hadn't bothered to proof because she'd worked so hard on the thinking and writing, and she knew I'd help her with the "errors" anyway. Ouch! I suddenly realized she hadn't grasped a basic expectation. She'd wasted my time if not hers by allowing me to help her correct what she could have corrected herself. When I receive a paper as "finished," I have a right to assume that any proofing "errors" are "errors" of ignorance, not inattention. When a student hasn't bothered to proofread thoroughly beforehand, the instructor gets a false impression and spends precious time on the unnecessary.

All of this applies to your writing group, as well. Collaboration works only if you complete your solitary work to the best of your ability. So, choose to proof. And allow plenty of time to accomplish it before proofing sessions with your group or instructor. If you do run out of time or energy, acknowledge such openly, take the consequences (if any), and make the best of the situation. Usually, honest discussion creates new possibilities. But please don't waste people's time.

What Solitary Methods?

Given that collaboration depends in part on solitary work beforehand, given your commitment to proofing, develop workable methods. "What's to develop?" you might ask. "Don't you just sit down and go over it?" Yes, if you're already good at it. But many college students aren't so good at it when they enter, and they need guidance in selecting and practicing workable methods, especially if they're good readers.

We read differently for different purposes, but READING—whether silent or aloud—concerns itself with meaning. When reading aloud, you read to present the language meaningfully to the listener. When you read silently, your eyes move across the print as swiftly as possible while still drawing up the meaning. You're not concerned with the graphic details of the text except as they help you express or grasp meaning.

When PROOFREADING, however, you're concerned with the graphic details of the text. You're searching for any inappropriate choices in grammar, spelling, punctuation, or other mechanics that might distract your reader's attention from your intended message. If you're a good silent reader, your eyes move too swiftly for good proofreading and must be trained otherwise.

In proofing, it's useful to sloooooow waaaaaaay down, pronounce the words a-loud syl-la-ble af-ter syl-la-ble, and examine each l e t t e r, each space, each mark. I sometimes run my pen along the sentence very slowly and make my eyes stay with my pen instead of   jump ing ahead   like they   always want to.

It's hard to think about meaning, read aloud, and concentrate on graphic details all at once. That's what proofing requires. When you train yourself to do it, you'll detect and be able to correct many more "errors" than before. Mark anything you're not sure of. Create possibilities for discovering what you know and don't know about written language. (Somehow I made it all the way through college before real-izing that *insight* is not *incite*.) "Correct" what you can on your own.

Using a Cassette Recorder

As with editing, I suggest a cassette recorder to help train yourself to proofread. You record yourself reading your paper aloud at a slow but natural pace. While lis-tening to it play back, you follow along with your pen, examining the text with your eyes. This technique enables greater visual concentration on the graphic details of the text. Why? Because your attention no longer needs to be divided between read-ing aloud and searching for "errors." Something else happens, too. If you've left words out of the text, you'll put them back in unconsciously when reading aloud into the recorder. You'll hear them and see their absence during the playback. After training yourself and practicing for a few weeks or months with the cassette recorder, as well as with your instructor and your group, you'll have improved your ability to proof your texts without the machine.

Observing Your Own Set of Proofing Issues

Each student displays a unique set of proofing problems that tend to show up over and over. Even a student who claims to be "poor in grammar" usually displays relatively few types of error. These same few types showing up over and over can create the appearance of an overwhelming array of separate problems. For example, at the end of a group proofing session, a student counts twenty-four errors that s/he failed to detect when proofing beforehand. Understandably, s/he may fall into discouragement or hopelessness about "grammar." So as not to lose hope, s/he needs guidance in understanding how these many errors may be sorted into a relatively small number of categories. Addressing one category at a time makes the job of resolution more manageable. Following are the eight types of error that show up over and over in this particular student's writing. S/he

1. Runs together two sentences with just a comma between them.

2. Puts quotation marks around the title of her paper.

3. Writes *it's* instead of *its*.

4. Writes, *Chuckling at the irony in almost every paragraph, the story "Good Country People" by Flannery O'Connor combines ironic humor and serious commentary about human behavior.*

5. Doesn't adhere to Modern Language Association guidelines for documentation; when citing a page number, writes *(O'Connor, pg. 13)*.

6. Puts the comma outside the quotation marks.

7. Sometimes uses incomplete sentences.

8. Sometimes puts in a comma or semicolon where s/he happens to take a breath.

Occurrence of these eight types just three times each could result in as many as twenty-four errors total. Understandably, the student could fall into discouragement, further convinced s/he's "poor in grammar," condemned to fail.

Using Your Writing Handbook

But let's consider the reality. Items 2, 3, 5, and 6 are fairly simple matters to resolve with the aid of the writing handbook:

2. Titles. Don't put quotation marks around your own title unless it's a quote from someone else. (Consult the writing handbook to learn the distinction between quotation marks and italics [or underlining] for various titles.)

3. *It's* and *its*. *It's* always means *it is* and nothing else; *its* is possessive like *his*. (See the handbook's glossary of usage.)

5. In-text citations. A page number cited in the style prescribed by the Modern Language Association for documentation appears like this: (O'Connor 13) or (13).

6. Comma and quotation marks. The comma normally goes inside: ,"

With at most an hour's work, the student in question can master half the list of eight types of proofing problems, leaving just four types. I admit they're more difficult to attend to:

8. Placement of comma and semicolon. S/he can consult the handbook for illustration. Even if s/he gets bogged down in the grammar lingo, s/he can read the examples aloud and observe conventional uses of these marks as guides for the reader. With coaching from the instructor and group, s/he can also learn to hear the unconscious voice patterns in our speech (not breathing patterns) that actually signal a comma or period—one kind of break or another. Most of the time, a semicolon is more nearly a period than a comma.

1. Running two sentences together with just a comma between them. S/he can learn (as immediately above) to read aloud and detect a fuller break than a comma break—s/he can learn to detect a voice pattern signaling a period or semicolon. (The handbook has a section illustrating the *comma splice* and how to correct it.)

7. Incomplete sentences. S/he can take a similar approach. S/he reads each sentence aloud, listening and considering the meaning. An incomplete sentence read by itself sounds and feels incomplete. (The handbook contains a section illustrating the *sentence fragment* and possible corrections.)

4. *Chuckling at the irony in almost every paragraph, the story "Good Country People" by Flannery O'Connor combines ironic humor and serious commentary about human behavior.* S/he can learn to read what the words actually say as against what s/he intends for them to say. Here, the words actually suggest, ludicrously, that the story chuckles: *Chuckling, the story . . . .* S/he intends to say that the reader chuckles. When writing the sentence, s/he neglected to include right after the *chuckling* clause, the person who's chuckling. To work, such constructions usually need reconstruction: *In her story "Good Country People" Flannery O'Connor combines ironic humor and serious commentary about human behavior. I chuckled with almost every paragraph.* (The handbook includes a section illustrating the *dangling modifier* and how to correct it.)

With thoughtful attention, the whole list can be mastered in a few weeks. Not that such habits of thought and language can be changed overnight. Chances are, the student will continue to write some of the same stuff. But because of new awareness and attentiveness at the proofing stage, s/he'll detect them and invite coaching as needed in learning to correct them. Ongoing involvement in writing and collaboration engender natural growth.

Natural Grammar

Natural grammar is the grammar you've learned to use in hearing and speaking your native language. You weren't *taught* your native language. John Holt, a thoughtful observer of language development, says that if infants had to be *taught* their native language, they'd never learn it. It's too complicated. Many twentieth-century theorists and researchers on language observe that we're born with the innate brain power and circuitry to *acquire* our native language without being *taught*. As infants and young children, we mainly *learn* it by being around our parents and others as they speak, gesture, and hear. We mimic them with our own utterances. We observe their responses to us, including their speech and gestures. In just a few years we develop the amazing ability to communicate with them in spoken language and its related behaviors such as body language. We learn what sounds right and what doesn't to the people in our lives.

Even more amazing, though, we don't just learn to say what we've heard others say. We don't just go around repeating other people's utterances. Mysteriously, our innate brain power and circuitry somehow enable us to make utterances that we've never heard anyone make before, utterances that the people around us understand. Our built-in circuitry combined with our ongoing observations of others enable us to make up utterances that are *grammatical* in our native language. Likewise, we're able to understand what others are saying even when they make utterances that we've never heard before. A likeable illustration of this remarkable human capacity comes from a British study that I read years ago. The researchers were observing the language development of infants and young children. As I recall, the researchers were seated in hearing-and-seeing distance of a small boy in a high chair eating breakfast with his parents. At his stage of development, the boy normally spoke utterances of just one, two, or three words. He would say things like "Mummy," "Daddy big," "Want milk," and "Doggy nice." That morning out of the blue he blurted out something like, "Mummy, please pass Daddy milk. Him thirsty." Clearly, this boy—and virtually every human child—displayed evidence of a wondrous built-in and acquired natural *grammar*. Somehow he was able to speak two understandable sentences much more complicated than he'd uttered before, sentences that embody basic grammatical structures that he hadn't been *taught* in any direct way. Of course, as we develop, we also take advantage of direct learning from our parents, teachers, and others. We continue to refine our linguistic abilities throughout our lives. Dr. Martin Luther King, a highly educated man, could speak brilliantly and beautifully in various "dialects" of English, one for a speech at, say, Harvard, another for a sermon in his home church, and yet another for talking with downtrodden civil-rights workers.

My point is that you already "know" much more grammar than may realize you. See what I mean? Right away you knew something was wrong with that last sentence. You knew it was ungrammatical for me to say "may realize you." If you've grown up hearing and speaking English, then you already know hundreds, even thousands, of language cues and structures. Otherwise people wouldn't understand you, and you wouldn't understand them. You don't have to know "school grammar" as such to become a good proofreader. You mainly have to learn to apply to your writing the natural grammar that you already know plus some visual refinements that you do have to learn directly. Of course, writing is not the same as speaking. And reading is not the same as hearing. But writing and reading do use the same basic system of natural grammar—represented visually. If you've been reading and writing since the age of five or six, then you've also acquired a lot more than you may realize about the appearance of written language.

I'm reminded of a young man who came to our college learning center for help. "My composition teacher says I'm a good writer but a poor proofreader," he explained. "I need lots of help with my grammar." When I asked him to explain his method for proofing and correcting his writing, he said, "I usually just read over it." "Show me," I said, "with the paper you've brought to work on." He *read* over it as though he was reading it for meaning rather than *proofreading* it for errors, and he missed all of the errors I saw on the first page of his essay. I showed him how I proofread, very slowly and deliberately, saying each word aloud (or at least aloud to myself). When he tried it again, he found eleven errors out of thirteen on the first page. He was of course delighted to learn he didn't really need much help with his grammar. He needed mainly to practice the craft of proofing as something quite different from reading just for meaning. He needed mainly to learn to use what he already knew about spoken and written language.

School Grammar

In studying "school grammar," we learn mainly to identify and name the "parts of speech," the "grammatical structures" in which they occur, and many other elements of grammar, usage, punctuation, and mechanics—in sentences that have already been written. It can be useful to know school grammar as one tool for helping us proofread. I wish everyone did know it. Then we could all speak about language in similar terms such as *nominative of address, coordinating conjunction, dependent clause, gerund, dangling participle, subjunctive mood, future perfect tense,* and so forth. If everyone knew in the same terms how to identify and name an *introductory adverbial clause,* then it would be a lot simpler to use a typical writing handbook. It would be possible, then, for nearly every student to understand such a handbook prescription as "Usually place a comma at the end of an *introductory adverbial clause.*"

In 1967, when I first began teaching in college, our English department expected the first semester to be mainly a course in school grammar. The idea was, as above, that if students knew it, they would then apply it in their writing during the second semester and thereafter. I was a good school grammar teacher, and I did my very best to help students learn to identify and name the parts and structures and other related matters. My experience, however, was that whatever they'd learned didn't show up much in their writing and proofing, even though I'd always tried to integrate their grammar study with their writing. As I read studies of this matter over the years, I learned that many other teachers and researchers were discovering the same problem.

Now, I'd grown up learning school grammar. By high school I could diagram virtually any English sentence, label everything with its official grammar name, and explain the stuff to my friends who hadn't been drilled in it as I had. I do use my knowledge of school grammar as one tool for proofing my writing. But over time

I've also observed that when I'm writing, refining, and especially proofing, that "artificial" knowledge is secondary or even tertiary to the other tools I use—more natural tools. In addition, in my thirty years of teaching college students, I've worked with hundreds of students who didn't know a lick of school grammar but who became competent or superb proofreaders as they learned to attend thoughtfully and naturally to the proofing process.

A Comma to Prevent Misreading

When I'm writing a sentence, I like placing a comma where I just did. The first part of the sentence I just wrote is called, in school grammar, an *introductory adverbial clause*. But I don't insert the comma because of the school grammar prescription that we should usually place one at the end of an *introductory adverbial clause*. I insert the comma for two better reasons. One is so the reader will pause momentarily instead of reading merrily onward and getting balled up trying to figure out where and how the first part of the sentence relates to the second part. I insert the comma to help the reader not misread the message. Without the comma as a signal to pause momentarily, the reader would probably go on and think I was going to say something like, When I'm writing a sentence I like, placing [it snugly in its paragraph feels as natural as waking with the sun.] The comma becomes just as important as the words and structures in conveying intended meaning. The reader shouldn't have to back up and reread the whole sentence two or three different ways to grasp it. The comma is like a good road sign. It tells you where you're going.

Natural Voice Contours and a Comma

The other reason I insert the comma is even deeper and more "natural." When I'm proofing a sentence, I like placing a comma where I just did because in reading the sentence aloud (or aloud to myself), I notice two distinct occurrences in my voice. During the second syllable of *sentence, -tence,* my voice pitches downward quite dramatically and then arcs upward, something like this:

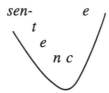

As my voice arcs upward, I expend breath to end the word in a sound something like *suh*. Right after that final sound, my voice pauses momentarily. This brief pause is the second of the two main vocal occurrences. Together, these two vocal occurrences—the dramatic pitching downward and arcing upward, and the momentary pause right afterward—are a natural way that we "punctuate" when we speak, so our listener can grasp readily the structure and meaning of what we're saying. In our writing, these same two occurrences signal a comma. When readers see the comma just ahead, they know intuitively to read the word *sentence* as I describe above, rather than some other way that would create another intended structure and meaning in the sentence. The upward arc and pause signaled by a comma create a short break and at the same time keep the reader poised for what comes next in the sentence.

When you read your writing naturally, read as you intend for it to sound, and record it on tape, the tape then reveals the natural contours of your voice—the pitches downward and arcs upward, the pauses, and so forth. Listening carefully, you can learn to *hear* a comma and *hear* other elements that are or should be in your text as clear signals to your reader. I invite you to seek coaching from your instructor in this simple, revealing process. My explanation may make it sound hard, but it's really quite natural and helpful.

Natural Voice Contours and a Period or Semicolon

There isn't space here to discuss the many possible vocal twists and turns that occur in our voices and listening. But I do want to approach one other: the period and semicolon. I talk about them together because when we read them aloud, they sound the same. And, they sound quite distinct from a comma. Learning to hear the difference between the sounds of a comma and the sounds of a period or semicolon can help you avoid common bugaboos of first-year college writers, such as the dreaded *comma splice, run-together sentence,* and *sentence fragment.* This trio is so common and so dreaded that most college writing handbooks include a section on each. Even if you don't understand the language of school grammar, you can gain a lot from the handbook by studying the examples and applying them in your own proofing process, both alone and with your group.

As well, you increase your chances of success by using your natural tools, by learning to *hear* the differences between a comma, which sounds one way, and a period or semicolon, which sounds another way. Read the following sentence(s) aloud and listen to your voice contours, especially surrounding a comma or semicolon or period:

Laura is usually a democrat; however, in the last gubernatorial election she voted for George Allen.

Laura is usually a democrat. However, in the last gubernatorial election she voted for George Allen.

Notice what happens in the last syllable of *democrat, -crat,* and on through the semicolon or period. Your voice pitches downward sharply and stays down. At a comma, your voice pitches down and arcs back up. But with a period and semicolon it stays down, something like this:

Your voice then emphasizes the "downness" with a definite pause that is slightly more pronounced than the pause for a comma. The "downness" and distinct pause that occur in speech signal to the listener a temporary moment of completeness. In a written sentence, this moment is signaled by a period or semicolon, which serves the same purpose for the reader. Instead of feeling poised for the rest of the sentence, as with a comma, the reader gets a more definite sense of ending. Vocally, a semicolon and period sound the same. Visually, they are of course different. A semicolon in effect combines the distinct "endingness" of a period, which ends a sentence meaningfully, with the "poisedness" of the comma, which helps a sentence continue meaningfully. Writers generally use the semicolon to achieve two purposes: to separate two sentence units that could appear as two sentences, separated by a period, and at the same time to show an especially close connection between them.

Run-Together Sentences

For illustration of how this idea works in proofing, consider the following *run-together sentence (fused sentences)*, produced by a former student in college-prep writing:

The morning came it was June 1994.

What enables you to sense that something is wrong? As you first read the "sentence" aloud (or aloud to yourself), you and your voice probably read right past the word *came*, because the whole utterance appears visually to be one sentence. Somewhere past *came* you realize something's not right. When you go back and read the "sentence" again, you adjust your voice contours to fit what you've discovered. On the word *came* you naturally make your voice pitch downward and stay down, with a distinct pause, before speaking (or subvocalizing). *It was June 1994.* (When we read silently, we *subvocalize*. We "say" the words to ourselves in a "voice" created by our interaction with the text. Whether or not we move our lips, we don't speak aloud. When we read aloud, we're *vocalizing* rather than *subvocalizing*. Our voice contours are the same in both processes.)

If you were to punctuate the "sentence" to enable the reader to read it right the first time, you'd use a period or semicolon:

> The morning came. It was June 1994.

> The morning came; it was June 1994.

These voice contours are so natural to us in speaking and reading that we don't think about them we just use them.

We don't think about *th*   we just use them.
e
m

> We don't think about them. We just use them.

> We don't think about them; we just use them.

In writing—or rather in proofing—if you do learn to hear them and think about them, you'll be pleasantly surprised that you're not so "poor in grammar" as you might have thought. If you have trouble with the *comma splice, fused sentences,* and/or *sentence fragments,* you might practice with the examples in your handbook. You might read each example into the tape recorder and then listen back, even if you do know and use school grammar. In a proofing session with a partner from your group, your partner reads each of your sentences aloud slowly. You can listen to his or her natural voice contours and adjust your commas, periods, and semicolons to match them. Learn to use all the tools available, especially those right at hand.

Proofing on the Computer

I've become pretty good at seeing what's there on my computer screen, but I'm never satisfied that I've proofed a piece thoroughly until I've printed a copy on paper and gone over it very slowly and deliberately. While still at the screen, I run the spell-check, which highlights any questionable words, I make corrections as needed, and then I proof the whole piece before giving the print command. My new computer program checks spelling automatically as I type and puts a squiggly red line under any word the computer doesn't recognize. (When fastwriting or drafting, I try not to stop and make spelling corrections, but it's hard not to when I see that red squiggle.) One nice feature about the other system, which my program also has, is that the spell-check gives you a list of words, only one of which is the word you're trying to spell. You can actually improve your spelling by examining the features of each word and selecting the one you intend. When you do, the computer replaces the misspelled word in your text with the word spelled correctly.

Besides spell-check, there are many grammar-checks in use today, some of which can be both handy and annoying. They're handy because they call attention to features of your text that might need correction or rewriting. I say *might need* because you must make a choice. For example, the grammar-check might say, "This sentence has thirty-three words. You might want to divide it into shorter sentences." Perhaps so. But you can't rely on the grammar-check to make that decision. Some thirty-three-word sentences read well and should not be broken up. It depends. So, don't assume it's always right. Use it thoughtfully. It may be a regular, required element of your composition course. Also, your instructor may require a special procedure for proofing on the computer—alone, or with your group, or both. There are programs available now for collaborating at each stage of writing, and they continue to improve.

After I've proofed thoroughly on the screen and made corrections, I print a copy. I mark clearly any further changes needed, so I don't overlook them when I return to the computer to make final corrections. As I do, I check off each one on my printed copy. Then I make yet another copy and check it again until I'm satisfied it contains no proofing errors. Before leaving the computer, I save my document on the hard drive and on a floppy disk or CD.

Benefits of Proofing Together

Frankly, collaboration during the proofing stage has created a remarkable breakthrough for me as a teacher of writing and especially for my students. For years I struggled to find better ways to promote successful proofreading, and then—there it was: simple, natural, effective.

Collaboration helps each group member learn to see the patterns and correct the "errors" that show up. While certain "errors" do sometimes show up in the writing of more than one group member, a member can often see in another's text the "errors" that the writer was unable to detect.

One member sees that another tends to break up "if . . . then" statements with a period: "If we don't do something nationally about health care costs. Then fewer and fewer citizens will be able to afford it." (Notice the voice contours.) Another sees that *conscious* should be *conscience*. Another sees the difference between *it's* and *its*.

One advantage to collaboration in proofing is that each group member, as well as the instructor, comes to the table with biases about language and writing. The conventions of language vary and change. Different members of your group will have been taught or will have learned different ways of judging the same element. A variety of readers brings up many more possibilities than you could possibly notice on your own. Expect fireworks.

One partner will question your use of *I* in a paper. Another will advise you to use *I* because it's what you mean. One partner will question your use of contractions. Another will report that s/he's seen contractions used in professional journals. Your instructor can help resolve such issues, but even the instructor will have to make some decisions based, not on "rules," but on professional judgement. You may want an absolute answer and become frustrated sometimes because s/he tells you, " It depends on your audience and purpose."

Everyone agrees that *a lot* is always two words and *American* is always capitalized. But whether or not to address the reader as *you*, as I do in this book, depends on the situation. I've chosen to address you as *you* because I want you to experience me as someone who is talking with you directly. Though I'm aware some readers will be offended by the usage, I'm hoping most will embrace it. If not, I've made a poor choice. Many of your choices will require judgement, which will develop from active reading and writing and interacting with others.

A Group Session at the Proofing Stage

Let's assume you've proofed your own text as best you can, corrected what you can, and marked things you feel uncomfortable about but don't know how to resolve.

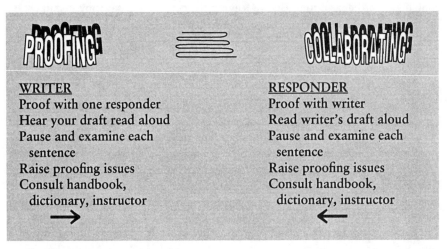

PROOFING		COLLABORATING
WRITER		**RESPONDER**
Proof with one responder		Proof with writer
Hear your draft read aloud		Read writer's draft aloud
Pause and examine each sentence		Pause and examine each sentence
Raise proofing issues		Raise proofing issues
Consult handbook, dictionary, instructor		Consult handbook, dictionary, instructor
→		←

You work with one partner at a time, sitting side by side so that both can see the same draft, though each may have a copy. (There are many advantages to all four group members proofing a draft together, but the process done thoroughly takes too long to complete four drafts in a class period. Two partners can usually finish two drafts with time left over, perhaps to work with new partners and time for the group to have a brief summary session.) You do one draft at a time—together—first one partner's and then the other's. When doing your draft, your partner reads aloud very slowly and deliberately one sentence at a time while you follow with your pen, examining the graphic features of the text with your eyes. Both pause after each sentence, go back to its beginning, and examine it silently and/or aloud.

Either partner calls attention to anything that seems questionable. Both talk about it and, as necessary, consult the dictionary, handbook, other group members, or the instructor. The point is to raise consciousness in both partners about proofing issues. The more discussion, the better. As a rule, a partner never writes corrections on the writer's copy. It's the writer's text, and the writer needs to decide what to change. You learn and remember more by physically making the change than if someone else does it. Also, it may be a form of cheating to allow someone else to correct your paper and for you to correct someone else's. In other words, there's a crucial difference between learning together and doing each other's work. If you go through and merely correct the other's text, your partner doesn't learn much, and neither do you.

GROUP SESSION—PROOFING STAGE

Leader   Convene the session.
           Remind each writer to give a copy to the instructor
             (if requested).
           Invite the raising of unsettled issues.
           Ochestrate resolution.
           Review procedures for the session.
           Designate partners.
           Call for each member's special intention for the session.

Member   Declare a special intention for the session.

                        (15 sec. each)

Partners   Sit side by side.
           Give copy to partner.
           Proof one draft at a time.
           Writer's partner: Read writer's draft aloud very slowly,
             pausing after each sentence.

Writer   Follow along with your pen.
           Discuss any feature that seems questionable.
           As needed, consult handbook, dictionary, other members,
             or instructor
           Writer: Make your own notes and corrections.
           Writer's partner: Don't write on your copy or the
             writer's copy
           When finished, proof the other draft by the same
             procedure.

GROUP SESSION—PROOFING STAGE *(cont.)*

IF CONFLICT ARISES

Leader	Talk constructively with whoever appears aggressive in the conflict. Help restore civility.
Advocate	Talk constructively with whoever appears defensive in the conflict. Help restore civility.

Leader	If there's time, have the group change partners and continue proofing.
Near end of period, convene the group to discuss how the session went. Invite the raising of unsettled issues. Orchestrate resolution. If necessary, consult your instructor. Close the session.
Writer	Follow your instructor's guidelines for making final corrections and other refinements.

Proofing: A Scenario

Imagine Maj-Britt sitting with her partner, Juan, beginning a proofing session. The two of them are side by side so both can see the same copy of her text. Each has a copy. Juan reads her text aloud one sentence at a time, starting with the title.

> *Maj-Britt: "Hey, Juan. I'm so glad your mother's better."*
>
> *Juan: "Yeah, me too. Things are pretty much back to normal at home. Whew."*
>
> *Maj-Britt: "I appreciate how you kept up with your work even though all that was going on."*
>
> *Juan: "Well, you guys have been great. Thanks for being so supportive."*
>
> *Maj-Britt: "Well, I've enjoyed getting to know you. And I appreciate how you all have accepted this older woman into the group."*

Juan: "Hey, what's a few years among friends?"

Maj-Britt: "I hear you. Okay, we'd better get started before the writing police come over and dog us. I'm never quite sure about my commas, so I'd appreciate any help you can give me."

Juan: "Well, I'm not too sure either, but we'll see what happens." John Red Elk: Medicine Chief and Love of My Life. "I see you've changed your title like we talked about. I like it because it focuses on John and your main theme. When I read it, I get two things: (1) He was the love of your life and (2) in your encounter with him you learned to love your own life, which is the way your piece ends. Nice. The punctuation and all seem fine."

Maj-Britt: "Good. You got just what I intended."

Juan: I am man first. "Shouldn't there be an a before man?"

Maj-Britt: "Normally, I suppose, but that's the way John talks. That's the way he said it, and I'm quoting him word for word, so I want to leave it like that."

Juan: "Okay. I see what you mean." I am chief. I am warrior. I have earned my power. I take what I want. No man tells me what to do! This was the passionate response of John Red Elk as he recounted the decision of his elders regarding his marriage to me. "No," they had said. "Shouldn't the comma go on the outside of the quotation marks?"

Maj-Britt: "I don't think so, but I'm not sure. Didn't Harrington say it always goes inside? Let's look it up."

Juan: "Here it is. You're right. The comma and the period go inside the quotation marks." "We forbid it." And then—much more gently—this strange mysterious man began talking of giving up his medicine, passing it on to another and living a quiet life with me.

Maj-Britt: "Does it seem okay to use dashes like that? Or should I use just commas?"

Juan: "It seems okay, but I'm not sure about the dash, so I don't use it much."

Maj-Britt: "Well, I looked it up, and it says you can use the dash to emphasize sentence elements like this."

Juan: "Well, it seems okay. Shouldn't there be a comma between strange and mysterious? One of my teachers taught me that if you can put and between two adjectives like this, then you should put a comma. It does make sense to say strange and mysterious, so I'd put a comma."

Maj-Britt: "Yeah, I see. It sort of sounds like a comma there when I say it: . . . this strange, mysterious man . . ."

Juan: "I think there should be a comma after the second part of that series, too, between passing it on to another and and living a quiet life with me. Harrington mentioned that journalists don't use that comma there but academic writers do—to separate the items in the series more clearly."

Maj-Britt: "Gotcha. I remember now." . . . talking of giving up his medicine, passing it on to another, and living a quiet life with me. "Yeah, the comma there does separate the three parts more clearly."

> *Juan: Sadness overshadowed his once powerful voice for he knew he could never leave his destined way.* "There should also be a comma in front of for. My writing handbook in high school said, I don't know why I remember this so clearly, 'Always use a comma before for when it means because.' Here it does, doesn't it? Also, our teacher said it's to prevent misreading. I remember reading your draft and thinking it was going to say something like a voice for his people, and I had to go back and reread it to get that it means because." *Sadness overshadowed his once powerful voice, for he knew he could never leave his destined way.*
>
> *May-Britt:* "Whew. I guess I need to get busy in the comma trenches."
>
> *Juan: My heart and spirit ached for him as he spoke of this peaceful life—this refuge from his medicine.* "I like the changes you've made to this sentence. It's simpler and somehow more, well, expressive."
>
> *Maj-Britt:* "Thanks. By the way, I changed talked to spoke because I'd already used talked above, and I thought spoke sounded better here."
>
> *Juan:* "Yeah, good. And the punctuation and other stuff seem fine. The dash creates a special connection between this peaceful life and this refuge. So, on to the next paragraph?"

Working like this with a series of partners develops your abilities and judgment as a proofreader. Each time you or your partner raises an issue, you both learn something. You tend to remember what you learn in this way—whatever your preferred style of learning—because it involves several styles: visual, auditory, tactile, and interactive. And once you get used to being with your group, working together enlivens the proofing process and helps keep the work going all the way to the finish.

Where's the Professor?

While my students proof together in pairs, I want to see them in consultation, looking things up, making every effort to resolve proofing issues on their own. I also want to see their hands pop up for my coaching. Sometimes I simply suggest where they might look in the handbook and remind them to call me back over if they need to. Other times, I do my best to help them see the proofing options and the best possible choice for the intended reader and purpose. In our two semesters of composition we concentrate mainly on academic writing, but we also compose, briefly, some personal narrative, fiction, and poetry. I recall one pair of students calling me over to ask the appropriateness of the raucous slang in a short story they were proofing. The student writer had done a good job creating a narrator who spoke in a distinct southern dialect. Her partner was concerned that the "misspellings" and "ungrammatical constructions" might not be suitable in a college class. Here was an ideal opportunity to discuss choices for a given purpose. Some of the dialect was overdone, I thought, so I showed them how to "suggest" dialect with less-noticeable "misspellings." Then I complimented the writer's creation of a believable voice to speak her story, and I moved on to help another pair. I enjoy this interactive, practical process of teaching and learning. It works best when you as the student seek help actively.

"Finishing" a Paper

Although a piece of writing can always be improved further, at some point you must move on to something else. Be sure to understand your instructor's expectations for "completed" pieces, whether placed in your portfolio or handed in. Your instructor has reasons for requesting or requiring a certain format, certain information to be included, and so forth. Some have to do with your learning such things as the Modern Language Association style for documentation or the expectation of academic readers that titles appear in a certain way.

Others may have to do with the instructor's own habits and practices. For example, a colleague of mine is left-handed. As an English professor, he reads and grades hundreds of papers. It saves him time and effort if his students staple their papers in the upper-right corner rather than the more common upper-left. He requires them to do so, and I can see why. Another colleague, also an English professor, doesn't want papers stapled but rather paper-clipped for easy removal. He likes the pages loose, just as editors do when reading a manuscript for publication. I require my students to staple in the upper-left.

Likewise, many of us want your name, the date, and other such information to appear in plain sight on the first page. It saves us time and trouble in locating what we need for our records. On the other hand, some teachers use a system of reading papers without knowing each author's name until after the evaluation is complete. These teachers might require students to include just a code number. Such individual quirks may seem odd or even unfair, because there are so many details for you to keep track of. But imagine yourself as a professor handling all the papers for several classes.

There's yet a third reason for following your instructor's directions: One element of education is the acquisition of both the willingness and the ability to follow directions and thus attend to certain details. In college, failure to do so, just as failure to proof carefully, might just signify sloppiness or laziness or insensitivity.

Grant yourself the time and wherewithal to present your work in its best form and in the form prescribed and expected by your instructor.

WRITER
Proof and correct further as needed

Maj-Britt's First Paragraph Proofed and Corrected

Red Elk: Medicine Chief and Love of My Life

"I am man first. I am chief. I am warrior. I have earned my power. I take what I want. No man tells me what to do!" This was the passionate response of John Red Elk as he recounted the decision of his elders regarding his marriage to me. "No," they had said. "We forbid it." And then—much more gently—this strange, mysterious man began talking of giving up his medicine, passing it on to another, and living a quiet life with me. Sadness overshadowed his once powerful voice, for he knew he could never leave his destined way. My heart and spirit ached as he spoke of this peaceful life—this refuge from his medicine.

HIGHLIGHTS

EMBRACE THE NECESSITY OF PROOFING

GRASP THE DISTINCTION BETWEEN PROOFING
AND READING

UNDERSTAND PROOFING AS CHOICES

PROOFREAD ALOUD SLOWLY

USE A CASSETTE RECORDER

USE YOUR WRITING HANDBOOK

USE THE COMPUTER
RUN SPELL-CHECK AND GRAMMAR-CHECK

BECOME AWARE OF VOICE CONTOURS
AND OTHER NATURAL PATTERNS

PROOF AS BEST YOU CAN BEFORE A
GROUP SESSION

WORK ENJOYABLY AND RIGOROUSLY WITH
YOUR PARTNER(S)

INVITE COACHING

FOLLOW YOUR INSTRUCTOR'S GUIDELINES FOR
PROOFING AND SUBMITTING FINISHED PAPERS

13

Odds and Ends

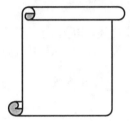

The Proof Is in the Pudding

Your paper is due in class today. Last night you finished up your final version. You checked your instructor's guidelines for submitting papers and made sure yours conforms. You printed it out, proofread it three more times to make sure it's perfect, made a few more corrections on the computer, and printed out a copy for your instructor and yourself. You saved the file on the hard drive and on a disk or CD, knowing you'll want to make more revisions after your instructor has read and returned it, probably with comments, perhaps with a grade. As you walk into class, your paper secure in your bookbag, you can't help feeling anxious. You've spent hours on your essay both alone and with your group. You've done your best to fulfill the assignment in every way. Now comes the real test. *What will the teacher think about it? What will s/he think about me? What grade will I get? How long will I have to wait? I have to make an* A *in this course.*

Grades. They're a fact of life at virtually every college and university. Ultimately, your instructor must submit your final grade for the course. The registrar's office will enter it into your file. It will appear on your transcript forever and ever. You'll have it sent to other colleges or universities you want to attend and/or to prospective employers. Your life feels on the line here, and so much depends on getting a good grade—no an A—on this very paper due this very morning in this #!*#!* comp course. Where's the justice? Where's the mercy?

> Prof: "Good morning, Hamid."
> Hamid: "Good morning, Ms. Tewksberry."
> Prof: "I really got what you were saying a couple of weeks ago about Emily Dickinson's playfulness, even in her somber poems. Not humor as in the lighter poems, but still a playfulness with language, an unexpected,

sometimes jolting choice of words that's analogous to what she does in the
lighter ones. Nice work. I'm looking forward to reading your paper."
     Hamid: "Thanks. Here it is." Gulp!

Somehow when others, especially authority figures, read our writing, we feel
exposed, vulnerable, anxious. If the reader is a professor who'll judge us with a
grade or a prospective employer who could offer us a job in that law firm, we feel
like pudding. Such readers, we feel, pass judgment not just on our writing but on us.
Our writing displays how and what we think, who we are in relation to our subject,
what attentiveness we show to things that educated people care about. There's an
old, albeit sexist, statement, "Style is the man." We are what we write. *Gulp!*

We're in This Pudding Together

For you as a student there is a lot at stake, and it helps if you can view your professor as an ally. S/he is. S/he wants very much for you to succeed. Otherwise,
s/he'd be doing some other kind of work, like sitting behind an elegant walnut desk
in a plush office overlooking Central Park, making a fat paycheck wisely investing
other people's money. Teaching first-year writing to college students is demanding,
sometimes frustrating, intriguing work. For me it's a privilege to guide students in
their growth as writers. I see writing—in harmony with other matters of language—
as the cornerstone of education. Good writing opens doors in college study and
nearly any career. Your professor is passionate about language and fine writing,
from essays to poetry, and s/he wants to share the passion and knowledge s/he's
acquired through years of study, writing, and appreciative reading. S/he wants to see
in you and your writing what s/he knows to be primary for your success.

S/he's your advocate, guide, mentor, and teacher. S/he's also your judge and
jury. Consider his or her potential conflict within. You've been struggling to make
an A. You want to be a good writer. You want to go to law school. You need high
grades. Your instructor understands your goals and needs. S/he does whatever s/he
can, within the bounds of the writing course, to support and guide you. S/he wants
you to make an A, just as I'd be delighted if every one of my students did. S/he's
reading your essay on Emily Dickinson's playfulness with language in the somber
poem "There's a certain slant of light":

> There's a certain slant of light,
> On winter afternoons,
> That oppresses, like the weight
> Of cathedral tunes.
>
> Heavenly hurt it gives us;
> We can find no scar,
> But internal difference,
> Where the meanings are.

None may teach it anything,
'T is the seal, despair,—
An imperial affliction
Sent us of the air.

When it comes, the landscape listens,
Shadows hold their breath;
When it goes, 't is like the distance
On the look of death.

S/he's impressed by your observations about Dickinson's choice of words—
tune, for instance, such a tiny-sounding word for the resounding airs of a pipe organ
in a grand cathedral. S/he appreciates your insights on how such words affect the
reader. S/he's impressed by the focus, arrangement, and development of your essay
as well as the clarity of presentation. You've quoted and discussed cogently several
illustrative examples. S/he can feel in your writing your fascination and appreciation
for Dickinson's artistry. At the same time, however, s/he detects some rough spots
in your transitions from paragraph to paragraph and some word choices that seem
clear but ordinary, word choices that stand out because the essay is generally well
written. Also, s/he discovers two sentences run together with just a comma
between—two *comma splices*—and a few other proofing oversights. The professor's responsibility is to grade on overall achievement measured on a scale of professionally determined expectations for first-year college writing. Perhaps
reluctantly (s/he likes the essay in so many ways), s/he assigns the necessary and
appropriate grade of B-. *Gulp!* Both of you were hoping for better. B is a respectable
grade, but it doesn't feel good enough given your plans.

*Why didn't my proofing partners catch those silly errors? Why didn't my group
see those "rough" transitions and those "ordinary" word choices? We've all worked
so hard on our papers and now this.*

B-. *#!*#!*. What do I do now? I made lots of A's in high school, but now I can't
buy one.* Perhaps not. An *A* in college writing is hard to come by. So is a B. In this
case the professor has appreciated the essay in many ways and, to my way of thinking, imagined it as potentially deserving of an A. It needs further work. *Doesn't the
work ever stop?*

The Work Goes On

These days, I'm pleased to say, many teachers and English departments have
designed courses that encourage the work to continue, even on papers that have
been turned in and graded. I'm not saying that all departments and teachers should
do so. But many do. There are good reasons why some don't. Even if your professor doesn't allow you to rewrite after the papers have been graded, my guess is that
your final grade will reflect your achievement as a writer at the end of the course.
You might get a C+ on the first paper, a C on the second, a B on the third, a B- on

the fourth, an A- on the fifth, an A- on the sixth, and so forth. In the dark ages when I was in college, writing teachers tended to average the grades for the whole term. If so, you probably would end up with a B. Nowadays, because most of us grade on ultimate achievement as a writer (not because we've succumbed to so-called grade inflation), it's more likely you'd get a B+ or maybe an A, depending on the details of the course requirements and how you've met them. We tend to understand better than we used to that writing is like a sport. In tennis class it's how well you play at the end that determines your achievement. In the beginning you whacked most of your serves into the net. By the end you serve in-bounds 80% of the time and even score some aces. The tennis teacher doesn't *average* your marginal performance at the beginning with your stellar performance by the end. In your writing course, no matter where your grades fall at present and no matter what system your instructor uses, accept the realities of grading and continue to improve until time runs out. View your professor as an ally and trust that the grades you receive are determined with professional judgment and fairness to all.

English departments and individual writing teachers, as it should be, develop their own best ways of collecting and evaluating student writing. Some professors have each student keep a portfolio of the work for the term and at the end read the portfolio to evaluate holistically the student's achievement overall. Some, even, invite the student to select a certain number of papers to be evaluated that represent the best work. Of those using such a system, many teachers don't grade individual papers along the way. They comment on each main piece of work and guide the student toward further improvement, desiring that the emphasis be on writing and not on grades. Also, many such teachers believe that a grade on an individual paper, especially early in the term, is not a useful indicator to the student or the teacher of the student's actual abilities and probable achievements as a writer by the end of the course. When I was at Duke in 1959, many potentially good college students earned grades of F or D on their early papers. The teachers, rightly, graded on the same standard at the beginning as at the end, so students could learn what was expected of a college writer. Most of us had gotten good grades in high school, and those early grades were quite an eye opener—or worse. They were pretty discouraging. Those who toughed it out eventually learned how to meet the rigorous expectations, but it wasn't a good system (although for its time, it was a first-rate program). We weren't guided in developing our papers. We weren't allowed to rewrite graded papers. The grades from beginning to end were averaged. And those harsh early grades smacked us like a sucker punch.

Whatever your instructor's system, when you receive back a paper, of course you look at the grade if there is one. But also study the marks and comments. Look for patterns in your strengths and weaknesses. Take the compliments seriously and build on them in future writing. If the transitions from paragraph to paragraph are rough, look up *transitions* in your writing handbook and get some pointers. As you work to improve the transitions in the essay you just received back, realize you're learning an essential element of good writing. Read your essay from start to finish and see if you don't notice the implied, intended connection from the end of one paragraph to the start of the next. Good transitions are *deep* transitions, built from the thought process, enabling the reader to understand what may be logical but unexpected connections. Try out some different ways of rewriting the passages in question and see what happens. Good transitions are a matter of thoughtful *feel.*

Likewise, if there are two *comma splices,* sentence errors that college students must learn to overcome, read the *comma splice* section in your handbook, study the examples, use a tape recorder, and make sure you apply the principles in correcting your current paper and in conducting future proofing sessions alone and in your group. If your group members didn't catch them either, then they need work on the *comma splice,* too. Remember that if you approach such a problem together, not only do you increase your chances of solving it, but you also increase your chances of applying the solution in the future. One of my most satisfying learning experiences as a college student was a study group for a botany course. (This was after I'd flunked out of Duke and was now paying my dues and completing my undergraduate degree at another university, where I majored in English and minored in biology.) We four guys would get together twice a week for about three hours to review the concepts and what seemed like rain forests of information to learn. I enjoyed the process, I came to a clearer understanding of things I hadn't understood, and I planted the material in my long-term memory. All four of us earned an A.

So, if you've tried on your own but just can't understand or accomplish something that your instructor marked or commented about, consult your group. Or consult your instructor. Or if your university or college has one, visit the writing center and get some tutoring. Some students, when they make a lower grade than they're comfortable with, feel self-conscious and become withdrawn. At the very time it would do them good to share their misery with a few trusted people and get help, they feel too embarrassed to do so.

This spring I'm working with a man nearly my age who continues to struggle with and improve his writing. Two years ago, he entered the college, took placement tests, and appeared in my college-prep writing class. He worked very hard every day. By the end of the first term, he wasn't ready for college-level writing, so he received a grade of R (*re-enroll*). He re-enrolled the next term, worked very hard every day, continued to make progress, and again received an R. The next term (with required permission) he re-enrolled yet again. He's a kind, jovial, insightful man with many friends of all ages at the college. His friends would ask him, "Why on earth are you signing up again with that same nut who flunked you twice already? Are you crazy?" "Yeah, I'm crazy. We're all crazy. Because I'm learning. I'm getting better. He dogs me and is never satisfied. How else am I going to get my education?" That third time, he made it, not by a big margin, but he made it. Last fall there he was in that same nut's college composition class. In the first term he worked very hard every day and earned a C, barely. This term, an introduction to literature and writing about literature, his struggle continues. He enjoys books and films. He manages a wheel-chair basketball team. He's discovered some fascinating qualities in Montresor, the narrator of Edgar Allan Poe's story "The Cask of Amontillado." He grew up in a rural household where there was lots of love but not much money or formal education. He'd worked all his life until recently, when a physical disability required that he do something else. He values education, clearly. I respect and admire him for many qualities. He helps countless other students face the music. They listen to him because, although some of them make better grades, he knows how to dig in and stay with something to the end—which in education is always a beginning. You can depend on him. He won't let you down. His writing group can always count on him to give and receive the very best he can. He reminds me of an American soldier in the Mekong Delta that a Vietnam vet told me about: "With him you knew you had a full partner when you went on patrol."

So, keep the work going—alone and together—until time simply runs out, whether or not you're allowed to rewrite and resubmit a graded paper for a higher grade. Whether or not you're expected to keep your papers in a portfolio for submission at the end of the course, go back to your earlier work and apply what you've now learned about transitions and comma splices. Rewrite and proof your essays as thoughtfully as you can. The more you practice your knowledge, the more likely it will stay with you. Too, your instructor is aware of who's really learning. When grade time comes, if you've been on the line between a C and a B, and now you're showing signs of strong *B* work, you'll probably get that *B*. At least you'll know you've done your best to improve and to help your group members stretch toward their goals, too.

A Fly in the Ointment?

There's also the sticky matter of a group that just won't click as a group. Although at least three members have tried hard, an apparent clash of personalities now feels impossible to overcome or live with. You've talked things over a few times—or tried to—and have sort of decided that the problem stems mainly from one person. You. You're a real loner by nature and don't want even to imagine yourself as a group player. You were a good, independent student in high school, and you liked it that way. You're always prepared. Your writing is pretty good, and it's improved some in just a few weeks, but not because you're listening very attentively to group responses. You sort of like to write, it's something to do alone, and you've been working at it mainly alone. You give half-hearted responses and keep quiet as much as possible. You're unhappy. Your group is unhappy.

If the teacher knew of the problem, s/he'd be unhappy, too, as well as happy to learn of it and desirous of orchestrating a solution. The other members haven't talked with the teacher because they don't want to rat on you. They've come to understand something of your nature. They basically like you, but they don't like you as a group member because you don't pull your weight. They and you dread coming to class, where the other groups labor cheerfully. All four of you want to improve your writing and make good grades, but the future looms dark.

It needn't. Talk with your professor, either alone or with your group. S/he'll want to determine whether you really are a loner who just can't seem to work productively in a group or whether you're capable of it but unwilling. Do you know for sure yourself? Your professor does understand that while most students can learn to thrive in a work group and most need to do so as part of their education, a very few might wither and droop. In consultation with you, your professor can explain, indeed, whether the group work prescribed for the course is an absolute requirement for a passing grade. If so and if you think you can learn to work better in the group, you can get coaching and adapt tolerably and productively. If you and the professor are convinced you must work alone, then you might have to take the course later with a teacher who uses a different method. Or your professor might offer you the option of doing your papers on your own and taking your chances on grades. I make very few exceptions to the normal requirements in my own courses, but I do keep the option open for an extreme case. (I recall in a graduate seminar years ago a very shy, brilliant student who made A+ on more than one paper. She said virtually nothing all semester and was probably too shy to become a teacher. But she surely was a fine scholar and writer who didn't get that way because of a writing group.) If you leave the group, the other three can conceivably work as a trio, or perhaps another group needs to be reconfigured, too. Orchestration of writing groups sometimes involves flexibility. So, see what you can work out with your allies—your teacher and your group members. Don't be a fly in the ointment.

Bushwhacking

As I've been saying, developing as a writer and reader is some of the hardest work you'll ever encounter—also some of the most satisfying because you'll feel grounded for your further education, career, and personal life. Growth means change. Change comes hard. Not that it can't be enjoyable. It should be. But feelings of discouragement will pop up like prairie dogs. Right now I'm going through a personal crisis with my fiddling. I've discovered a better style of bowing that swings and rocks like I'd never imagined in my own playing. As I work on it, I can hear its possibilities, and they excite me. But I'm having to relearn tunes I've played for over fifteen years. In some ways it's like starting over. I ask myself, why didn't I get somebody to show me this bowing method when I first began? Of course, it does no good to wish the past different. In a jam session with friends, I try to incorporate my new style. But I can't play up to jam speed (fast!) unless I fall back to my old ways. I need time and patience and the belief that in a few more months I'll be scratching out tunes in my new style—up to speed.

You might feel discouraged because you come to college with what seems like inadequate preparation. Perhaps you didn't write much in high school, though you read some good books, and now it's writing, writing, writing. You're probably better "prepared" than you might think, if you learn to use what you do know. It's also a good idea to accept your limitations. I didn't begin playing fiddle until I was thirty-six, though I'd played guitar and sung traditional American songs since my junior year of high school. I keep scratching along, getting better and better, knowing that I'll never be a great fiddler because I didn't start when I was six or seven. Sometimes I'll meet a young player, maybe fifteen, who outplays me by a mile. But old-time music and education aren't supposed to be about competing with others. It's fine to admire someone else's capability and feel inspired toward self-betterment.

Too often, we measure ourselves against others and then feel beaten down by our own inadequacies. I try to accept my limitations and keep sawing away on my old fiddle. It's great fun and very satisfying—except when I let my awareness of limitations impede my joy.

Right now in your life, your upper limit in composition might be a B-, no matter how hard you work. The point is to keep churning forward and get the best education, career, and personal life you can. A grade of B in college is respectable, if not as desirable as an A. And the differences between a B and an A in writing may require a couple of years to overcome. Learning to focus, for instance, can be a long process of trial and error. You think you've got a good focus, you write a whole draft, and then you realize yourself or someone else tells you that it's too broad and unmanageable for such a short essay. So, you narrow in and redraft and redraft. Finally you get it. Still, you can't say with honesty, "Now I know how to focus." You may be more efficient in focusing the next paper. I hope so. But chances are, you'll have to draft and redraft and redraft that one, too. And so it goes. Even many professional writers have to allow themselves time, space, and patience to work through the writing messes they find themselves balled up in. Writing is like bushwhacking in the wilderness. There's always a fresh stand of brambles or a rhododendron thicket or a ravine. We make it through—or around—with an earned sense of satisfaction. In time we learn to face more productively whatever comes up. The same goes for work in a writing group. The most important lesson is to acknowledge our problems openly with those involved, cultivate mature conversation, and embrace the things that make us human.

HIGHLIGHTS

YOUR TEACHER IS AN ALLY

ACCEPT THE REALITIES OF GRADES

FACE YOUR LIMITATIONS

KEEP THE WORK GOING

WE'RE ALL IN THIS PUDDING TOGETHER

FIND ADVENTURE IN BUSHWHACKING

NOTES

NOTES

NOTES

NOTES

NOTES

NOTES

NOTES

NOTES